Blooming Small

Blooming Small
A city-dweller's garden

Sheila Jackson

Mean while the Mind, from pleasure less,
Withdraws into its happiness:
The Mind, that Ocean where each kind
Does streight its own resemblance find;
Yet it creates, transcending these,
Far other Worlds, and other Seas;
Annilihating all that's made
To a green Thought in a green Shade.

Andrew Marvell, from *The Garden*, 1681

The Herbert Press in association
with The Royal Botanic Gardens, Kew

First published in Great Britain 1994
by The Herbert Press Ltd, 46 Northchurch Road, London N1 4EJ
in association with The Royal Botanic Gardens, Kew

House editor: Brenda Herbert
Designed by Pauline Harrison
Set in Linotype Guardi
by Nene Phototypesetters Ltd, Northampton
Printed and bound in Hong Kong
by South China Printing Co. (1988) Ltd

A CIP catalogue record for this book is available from the British
Library.

ISBN 1-871569-64-8

Author's note
The scientific plant names used in this book are those currently
used in the horticultural trade. These are subject to change and
may not, in all cases, be botanically correct.

Contents

Introduction: A particular place

My garden in central London is smaller than small. It hugs the main railway line within half a mile of Euston station – a not very prepossessing situation. I first viewed it with a friend, who said a pot or two would help! Otherwise the ambience was agreeable, the surrounding houses are handsome, Regents Park is three minutes' walk away, the Grand Union Canal passes under a bridge at the end of the road and in the early morning, from the Zoo, the gibbons' clear call is borne on the wind.

The estate agent described a 'patio with planted area' – otherwise a cracked concrete yard approximately 28 × 18ft (7.75 × 5.5m) containing an area of clogged earth in which the builders had buried the rubbish from the conversion into flats of the substantial mid-nineteenth-century house. Even today fragments of linoleum and defunct electrical wiring work their way to the surface. Lime trees dripped gummily over all; but over the years, the railway authorities have relieved me of these, fearing that the overhanging branches might entangle with their trains.

Undeterred by the deep foreboding of friends, I moved in and without a tremor and only some rusty school botany behind me I set about making a garden – nothing ambitious: somewhere with a few plants in pots, backed by a delphinium or two, where I could sit and admire the flowers and tend and water them to the constant rumble of trains.

A young architect encouraged ambition and advocated landscaping. He masterminded the purchase of sand and cement and a load of old London stock bricks. Together we set about confining my mud patch with little walls of sitting height, foreseeing a future less busy than it turned out to be. The first step had been taken, a shape had arrived.

The friends who had predicted that nothing would grow had to be proved wrong, and before long my plot, well dug and fed, had begun to burgeon. It was obvious from the start that because of the restricted area of earth it would be necessary to rely a great deal on containers, and I set about obtaining some large clay pots and two simple urns of earthenware. The light was good; the railway is wide at this point and buildings are some distance away across the tracks, the house wall faces south-west and from midday to sunset the garden receives full sun. New lap fencing formed the boundaries. It did not take long to achieve a superficial prettiness with summer bedding in the pots and a few herbaceous plants from the local store in the bed – but this did not amount to a real garden, and I began to sense the pattern of something more interesting and rewarding developing . . .

The small size of the garden suited and pleased me. As an illustrator of books I am used to the small page and have been trained to have a seeing eye; to be inventive with colour and shape is part of my trade, and that important quality – a sense of scale – has developed with the years.

I needed my garden to be green all the year round so that the outlook from the house would at all times be leafy, and it was essential to clothe the surrounding fences so that I should be secretly enclosed. As time went on, the climbers I planted slowly covered the perimeter with a pattern of foliage. By disguising the edges in this way, the garden felt curiously extended rather than confined, suggesting that, beyond the curtains of green, there were more spaces to be explored. Once established, summer jasmine, *Clematis × jouiniana* 'Praecox' and the rambler rose 'Félicité et Perpétue' intermingled with evergreen ivies and, as a relief from the greens, *Artemisia arborescens* with silver filigree foliage, *Helichrysum petiolare* with felted grey leaves and *H.*'Limelight', a soft yellow-green, joined them and rambled through them in summer.

To achieve unity in a small area, colour needs to be both restricted and restrained so that the eye can wander gently from place to place without experiencing sudden jumps from one bright colour to another. It is important to avoid the fussiness of too many small-leaved plants and to include large and dramatic leaves. The plants were acquired gradually; there was no rush to buy, just a slow building-up of plants which were going to look well together and were right in this particular garden – and besides, I was no cheque-book gardener! As I needed more space, it became necessary to grow plants at a variety of levels – not just as climbers, but situated at different heights. The realization of the need for height and the use that can be made of it was the most important factor in developing the style of the garden.

Four handsome chimneypots over 6ft (1.8m) high came from our own roof, and I obtained three more standard ones. With a simple Victorian saucepan stand from a junk stall, I began to solve my need for different levels.

As the plants multiplied, more containers were needed to hold them, and these were banked together in order to avoid a neat array of pots set out like tombstones in a churchyard. With some good-looking bricks from discarded off-peak storage radiators and some slabs of unwanted marble it was possible to build shelves so that the containers could be grouped together at different heights. Eventually there were growing spaces from the tops of the tall chimneypots down to ground level where *Cymbalaria muralis* (ivy-leaved toadflax), *Soleirolia* and *Campanula poscharskyana* seeded themselves and began to invade some of the cracked concrete.

The south-west-facing house wall is divided by the french windows to my workroom. On one side, lit by bright sunshine, there is now a pot bank containing much that is silver and grey and steely blue, varied by some yellow leaves. Euphorbias have a home here, and a broom spills over in a waterfall of pale yellow pea flowers

in April. Behind this at the back, where a trellis hides unsightly pipes, more climbers serve to form a decorative screen.

On the other side of the window a vine, proudly and successfully grown from an eye, became a flourishing plant; this was when the arch or mini-pergola was added as a necessary support and it now frames the garden as the visitor enters by the side gate. To make the arch interesting in spring, a *Clematis montana* precedes the vine – both climbers were planted in the bed to give them space to spread their roots. Along the house wall, in the speckled shade, *Brachyglottis* 'Sunshine' grows as a climber mingled with *Solanum jasminoides* 'Album' and the frail climber *Dicentra macrocapnos*; a clematis from Tashkent has recently joined them, which I have yet to see in flower. Squeezed into the pots are a number of hellebores, strong leathery leaves contrasting with the feathery foliage of ferns and *Polemonium pauciflorum* (Jacob's ladder). The window is framed by two correas, each now 6ft (1.8m) high, covered in winter with small bells. Between the tall chimneypots are glimpses of two raised tubs holding hostas, foxgloves, pulmonaria and maidenhair fern – this is the woodland bit!

For many years the central concrete area remained open, until a pot bank facing south-east grew up round one of the smaller chimneys. The pots mostly contain small shrubs which do not need full sun – daphnes, sarcococca, a lace-cap hydrangea, and hostas; and here *Cestrum parqui* produces two crops of sweet-scented yellow flowers. Latterly many yellow subjects have been added to the garden (avoiding bright egg-yellows) since I realized how well they looked with the white and green flowers and the wealth of different-coloured foliage. A retirement present of a circular jardinière joined this central bank and is filled in summer with tender plants replaced in winter with small evergreens.

From a few pots set on a marble table, the third pot bank was developed; this moved about until it settled down facing due south, and had added levels; it includes the bog-loving *Darmera peltata* growing in a plastic kitchen bowl filled with water and well camouflaged!

Here, too, dark-leaved plants were introduced to weave their way into the background where *Hydrangea serrata* 'Preziosa' turns deep maroon in autumn.

One enormous advantage of gardening with so many pots is the resulting flexibility both in altering massed shapes and moving plants according to season, and this has helped greatly in arriving at the overall shape of the garden. Also the close proximity of the pots, standing one upon another, helps to keep the roots cool. It does, alas, mean that watering can become burdensome, especially as in many cases it has to be very specific.

The garden is given a feeling of unity by the use of many hostas and corydalis repeated in different areas to create a binding thread. The flowerbed, no longer sporting the delphiniums and standard 'Superstar' roses of early years, could still be improved – it becomes very unshapely in early autumn. Hellebores and epimediums retain their shapes well and I would not be without the increasing colony of *Polygonatum* (Solomon's seal) and *Smilacina racemosa*. Two hardy fuchsias, *F.magellanica* 'Alba' and *F.*'Hawkshead', continue flowering prettily until autumn.

After ten years, needing somewhere to protect plants in winter and having no room for a greenhouse, I had a

frame built on the outside of my bedroom window – a kind of wardian case (see page 73). Here, too, cuttings and seeds can be brought on. It has proved a most valuable addition to the garden and one with which any gardener short of space should experiment.

Because of its smallness I can be constantly aware of everything that is going on in the garden; it fulfils my taste for a few blooms that I can enjoy individually rather than extensive and floriferous beds and borders. Its restrictions and limitations have proved stimulating and rewarding and it has been an unending source of pleasure to me for twenty-eight years.

Drawing the garden

By recording with pen and pencil throughout the year the plants as they come into season, reference has built up of both present and deceased friends. While working on this book, these drawings have been extremely useful. Some have been drawn *in situ* in the garden; at other times pots or cuttings have been brought inside, where it is easier to concentrate more closely with the aid of a lens and a magnifying glass on a movable arm. These are neither botanical drawings nor flower paintings, but fall somewhere between the two, aiming at recording the character and growth of the plants and the ways I have found of using them in such a small garden.

Sometimes, when looking at beautiful and accurate representations of plants, one feels that they are frozen in time, as if there had been no growth before and there will be no growth after those hours in which the careful, painstaking image was put down on paper – unlike the work of John Nash and Charles Rennie Mackintosh, whose lovely drawings convey a feeling of continuous growth. I have tried to emphasize this feeling in making the watercolour drawings of my garden for the book. It has also been necessary to be very selective; the particular quality of a garden can easily be lost in a blur of colour or a busy representation of a mass of plants. Careful choice helps to retain shapes without losing plant characters, eventually arriving at a result that is sufficiently explicit.

The garden plan

The garden is situated on two sides of the house and is reached from the road by a flight of steps, from the top of which there is a pleasing aerial view of the side garden, hinting at the rich green-ness of this tucked-away oasis. The side garden has the character of a basement as it lies 6ft 6ins (2m) below street level; however, quite a lot of light reaches the area as the early sun floods it in the morning and a shaft of light strikes from the side gate in the afternoon, prettily backlighting the leafy grouping of pyracantha, jasmine and ivy. The pyracantha, now a considerable tree, and the summer jasmine make an impenetrable arch of greenery which gives total privacy from nearby houses and also screens the path to the side gate from intruders who might contemplate access to the back of the house. The only soil available is a square which hosts the pyracantha and this now is covered over with a pattern of stones. The area is well furnished with a variety of containers planted with shade subjects, many of them evergreen, and the wall opposite the windows is completely clad with ivy interwoven with jasmine so that the outlook is into a green haven, and leafy throughout the year. A white wooden trellis, unplanted, against the east-facing section of wall creates a patterned eye-stopper before the garden narrows into the passageway to the gate.

From the house there is access through the entrance door, or from the french windows of the sitting room, and there is a feeling of greenness invading the interior.

A water butt and outside tap are helpful when there is watering to be accomplished, and by the compost bin a storage and work area is convenient for both parts of the garden.

The back garden, which is the true garden, is not basement. It spreads along the back wall of the house, the aspect is south-west and there is light at all times and full sunshine from mid-day to sunset. The main railway line into Euston station runs in a shallow cutting and its width at this point means that

plastic water butt

houses do not cut out light or overlook the garden, and there is a surprisingly large area of open sky. With the exception of the brick-edged flowerbed, the ground area is well-worn concrete, sufficiently cracked to give an agreeable surface and now largely covered with containers. The low wall, built in the first year, now supports so many containers that there is little room for sitting. The two urns obtained at the same time, together with the row of large pots along the party fence, were the only initial planning and outlay. Subsequently the four tall chimneypots have become an important feature and the pot banks have built up gradually and been shifted a foot this way or that to make the best shapes and to provide space for movement around the garden.

The plan as it stands today has gradually evolved over twenty-eight years and although new plants and replacements may change some outlines, the basic arrangement now seems finite.

Gradual development is one way of arriving at a planned garden and has been the way used here. The garden and I seem to have grown and matured together. Others may prefer to plan all from the outset, satisfactorily; but when planning small, the

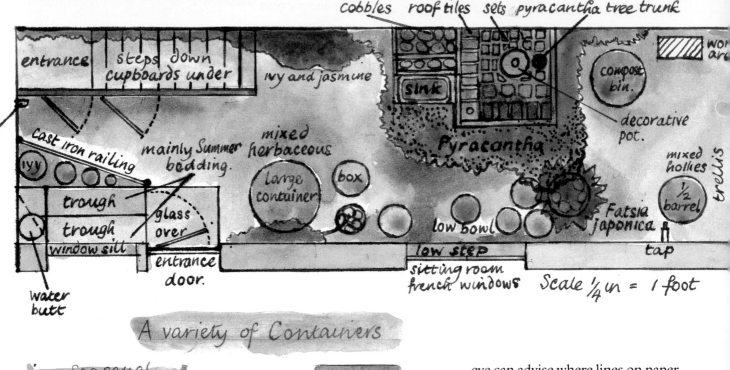

cobbles roof tiles sets pyracantha tree trunk

entrance

steps down
cupboards under

ivy and jasmine

sink

compost
bin.

decorative
pot.

won
are

Pyracantha

mixed
hollies

½
barrel

trellis

Cast iron railing

ivy

mainly Summer
bedding.

mixed
herbaceous

large
container

box

glass
over

trough

trough

window sill

water
butt

entrance
door.

low bowl

Fatsia
japonica

low step

sitting room
french windows

tap

Scale ¼ in = 1 foot

A variety of Containers

Seasonal
planting

Small bowl (composition)

Clematis macropetala
Lonicera pileata
Sarcococca
Arum italicum
Hostas.

Helleborus
T
trailers.

cut pot

Stachys lanata
Ajuga reptans
'Atropurpurea'

Large container (composition)

Square pot

various Ilex
Sarcococca
Acanthus

½ barrel

Euphorbia
characias sspwulfenii

Orange pot

Nicotiana
Sylvestris

Hostas

deep earthenware
container

earthenware trough

Ballota pseudodictamnus
Ruta graveolens
Ophiopogan planiscapus nigrescens
Oxalis triangularis

eye can advise where lines on paper
may be misleading, and devising this
garden has been like working on an
illustrated page, filling in the shapes
and colours very slowly.

Thoughts on pots

Pots can be very costly. For a special
feature I would advocate the purchase
of a really choice piece to be enjoyed
in the manner of a sculpture.

For general garden use, earthenware pots are better looking than
most others; they are not cheap, may
crack in a hard frost, or simply break
with careless handling. (Some garden
centres now sell a range of pots that
are guaranteed frost proof.) Composition containers and half barrels are
unaggressive, and at country sales it is
sometimes possible to pick up old
coppers – iron containers formerly
used for washing clothes – and other
domestic articles such as bread
crocks, milk churns and old stone

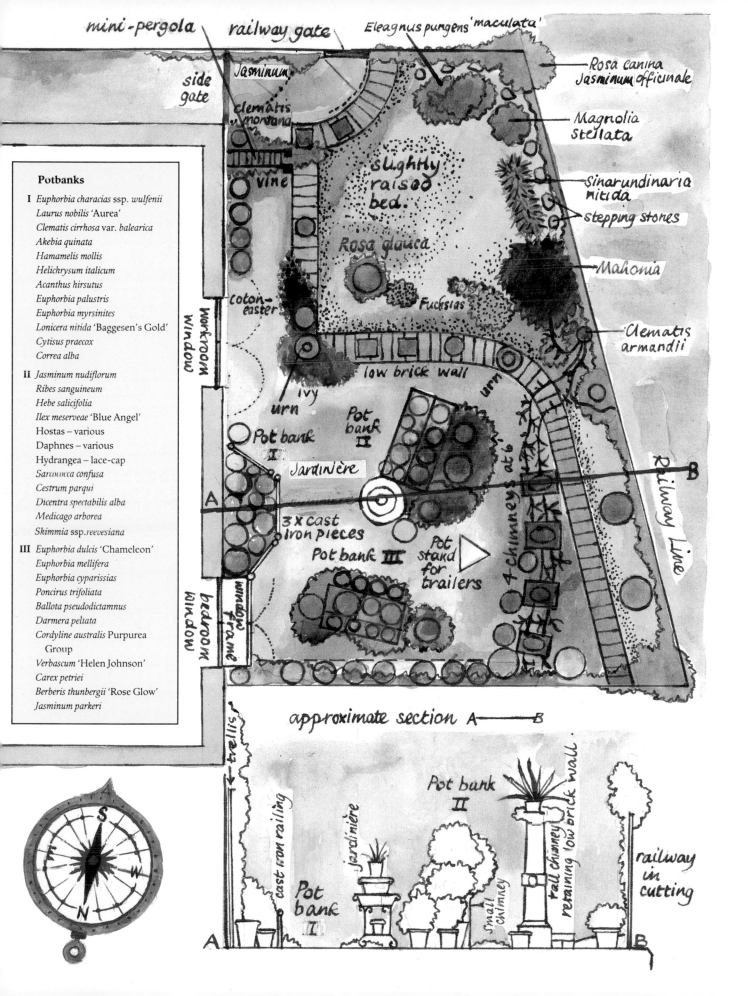

mini-pergola   railway gate   Eleagnus pungens 'maculata'

Jasminum

side gate

clematis montana

vine

Potbanks

I   *Euphorbia characias* ssp. *wulfenii*
    Laurus nobilis 'Aurea'
    Clematis cirrhosa var. *balearica*
    Akebia quinata
    Hamamelis mollis
    Helichrysum italicum
    Acanthus hirsutus
    Euphorbia palustris
    Euphorbia myrsinites
    Lonicera nitida 'Baggesen's Gold'
    Cytisus praecox
    Correa alba

II *Jasminum nudiflorum*
    Ribes sanguineum
    Hebe salicifolia
    Ilex meserveae 'Blue Angel'
    Hostas – various
    Daphnes – various
    Hydrangea – lace-cap
    Sarcococca confusa
    Cestrum parqui
    Dicentra spectabilis alba
    Medicago arborea
    Skimmia ssp. *reevesiana*

III *Euphorbia dulcis* 'Chameleon'
    Euphorbia mellifera
    Euphorbia cyparissias
    Poncirus trifoliata
    Ballota pseudodictamnus
    Darmera peltata
    Cordyline australis Purpurea
      Group
    Verbascum 'Helen Johnson'
    Carex petriei
    Berberis thunbergii 'Rose Glow'
    Jasminum parkeri

Rosa canina
Jasminum officinale

Magnolia stellata

Sinarundinaria nitida

stepping stones

slightly raised bed.

Rosa glauca

Mahonia

Fuchsias

Clematis armandii

Workroom window

coton- easter

low brick wall   urn

ivy urn

Pot bank II

Jardinière

Pot bank II

Railway Line   B

A

3 x cast iron pieces

Pot bank III

Pot stand for trailers

4 chimneys at 6

bedroom window

window frame

approximate section A — B

trellis

cast iron railing

Jardinière

Pot bank II

small chimney

tall chimney retaining low brick wall

railway in cutting

A   Pot bank II   B

January

sinks which are serviceable and decorative if used with judgement.

Many gardeners, working on a tight budget, will have to make do with some plastic pots. Providing it is not a replica of a fancy urn or bowl, a straightforward plastic tub, preferably in dark green, will be unobtrusive; and large plastic pots can be tucked into corners, surrounded by old bricks or hidden behind trailing plants. Dark brown plastic buckets with good drainage holes punched in the bottom make solid containers for shrubs, and are more substantial than large plastic flower pots. Plastic containers have the advantage of not drying out as quickly as those made of clay, though the latter may be discreetly lined with perforated polythene to delay evaporation.

DIARY

1 January – garden records

For the last ten years it has interested me to keep a reasonable record of the garden by making drawings of plants as they have come into flower and also using the camera for the same purpose as well as for photographing areas of the garden at different times of year. These drawings and photographs form useful reference material and provide simple garden records. Also, over ten years, the dates when plants came into flower have been logged, showing an interesting pattern of the seasons and considerable variation from year to year. More recently the dates of acquisitions have been added and there are a few notes – alas, too few – commenting on the vagaries of the weather. Browsing through the book today I wish the details had been more extensive, and I have made a New Year's resolve to do better in future. From another book a few pressed flowers fell from the pages and I regret I have not made more effort in this way too, for there is

a news paper

press with wing screws

also a place for pressed flowers as part of a garden record. Some sheets of newspaper, two pieces of plywood and some pressure will suffice as equipment for any number of pressings.

Taking time to look through the amassed material prior to putting it into some sort of order, I find drawing is so much more explicit than photography – the photograph presents an attractive image whereas the drawing fully explains the plant. It made me realize the importance of *looking* and how few people do it well. Artists are trained to look and to cultivate a visual memory, although many of them tend to be rather casual about it. It is an ability that stands one in good stead when gardening, and gardeners would do well to cultivate it; it helps greatly in the recognition of plants, seedlings and seeds, and diseases, pests and even minor discomforts of plants are observed in the early stages and can be quickly rectified. The observation, 'I hadn't noticed', is the mark of a gardener with a lazy eye!

Making use of a lens opens up a whole new world of vision and develops an appreciation of structure and design in plants, and a walk round the garden with a lens or a magnifier such as a linen tester reveals a whole new world of delight.

folding
linen tester

botanist's
lens

DIARY
*15 January – tidying the work corner
– on being patient*

Tidying the work corner is a task to be accomplished on a fine January day in anticipation of all the garden jobs that will shortly be mounting up.

However small the garden, it needs a space set aside for storing sacks of compost and sand, not to mention the mound of flower pots and seed trays that constantly accumulate. In gardens where there is more space, all kinds of garden detritus are often tossed in grotty and ever-mounting heaps with an out-of-sight-out-of-mind attitude. Not so for the owner of the small plot, who must keep his work area strictly within bounds. It is always difficult to throw away old pots, but it must be done; and canes and stakes need sorting into bundles, the useful link stakes confined tidily to a box. Clearing and tidying and general garden hygiene will help to keep down pests. As I have very little covered storage space, sacks, watering cans and pressure sprayers are stacked and covered with a small tarpaulin to keep them dry as well as making the area as presentable as possible.

At this time of year, the necessity for patience should be emphasized. Apart from the early flowering shrubs the garden is mostly at a standstill and

link stakes & Y stakes

may yet experience the coldest days of winter which so often arrive in February and March.

It is tempting, if there is a spell of good weather, to remove some unsightly plant protection or to go out with secateurs and cut back 'old wood' only to find the twigs green and obviously alive inside. During these early months, plants that stay dormant (especially after a cold spell) should not be assumed to have died, which is often the reaction of the impatient gardener. One of the main mottoes of gardening is to wait a little longer – life springs, if not eternal, sometimes rather late! A garden is no proper place for the impatient person.

January

January scents

Although their flowers are small – even inconspicuous – many of the winter-flowering shrubs are sweetly scented. The best position for them is near to doors and windows, where pleasing whiffs can be enjoyed as one passes to and fro; an added advantage of a small, sheltered garden is that all scented plants can be appreciated to the full. The tiny flowers of the sarcococcas, hardly more than a bunch of stamens, will fill the air with great fragrance. Known commonly as winter box, these evergreen bushes have well-shaped tiny leaves and the flowers are followed by fat berries, black in most varieties, which are held for a considerable period. The variety *S.hookeriana* has slender pointed leaves and in the form *S.h.* var. *digyna* they are carried on a purple stem. As these small shrubs, rarely exceeding 4ft (1.25m) in height, are very slow-growing they should find a place in every tiny garden. They will propagate slowly but reliably from cuttings and frequently seed themselves.

Lonicera fragrantissima, winter honeysuckle, covers itself with a long succession of small, pinkish-white scented flowers borne on bare twiggy branches if the winter is hard or among leaves when conditions are less harsh. This can grow into a very big bush and needs severe pruning after flowering to keep it shapely in a small space. Mine grows in a large pot just outside the workroom window so that I can capture all the heady fragrance on a miserable winter day.

Also scented, but less powerfully, *Hamamelis mollis* is one of the witch hazels: the masses of spidery yellow blossoms hug the bare stems tightly. It too can grow large, but this one has not yet outgrown its position in seven years and seems happy although confined to a pot. The leaves when they appear are undistinguished but turn a lovely yellow in autumn.

The little known *Abeliophyllum distichum* is another early flowerer with fragrant, small flowers on stick-like stems – in fact, after leaf-fall in autumn no bush could look more dead!

Charming and cheerful from Christmas to March, the winter jasmine, *Jasminum nudiflorum*, bears yellow flowers along arching green stems which are still bare of leaves. Severe pruning at the end of flowering will ensure a good display next year.

Because any crocus here is decimated by birds I regretfully no longer grow them, but the tuberous rooted perennial *Eranthis hiemalis* (winter aconite) pushes its way through evergreen ground cover, providing bright yellow cups surrounded by green frills; and in sheltered corners winter pansies bravely produce a few flowers.

Meanwhile the *Mahonia japonica* (Bealei Group) which began its flowering period in late autumn is now in full display and the garden is filled with its lovely lily-of-the-valley fragrance.

Jasminum
nudiflorum

Viola

Hamamelis
mollis

Sarcococca hookeriana

Abeliophyllum
distichum

Lonicera
fragrantissima

Eranthus
hiemalis

Sarcococca
ruscifolia

Sarcococca
humilis

February

The garden is full of birds, who would feed all day if there was a sufficiently lavish supply of food. They come to the transparent plastic feeders held on to the workroom windows with suction cups, and also to the fat-ball suspended on the pot stand. They are a delight to watch, particularly as they stack, fluttering, awaiting their turn to land. They fill the garden with activity and interest in these dark, dull days. A pair of robins, a pair of blackbirds, wrens, dunnocks and sparrows are regular visitors; but alas, no longer any tits, the ever-increasing numbers of noisy jackdaws and jays have driven them away.

The berries on the bushes have long since been gobbled up, but the wrens and dunnocks scour the twiggy growth of the Russian vine for insects. The moment I open the french windows the robins are at my feet hoping I may turn over some soil, and a flock of sparrows and dunnocks line up in

an overhanging tree in anticipation of the feeders being topped up!

This is a good time to start clearing leaves from the flower bed, especially mahonia leaves which is a particularly prickly job; they harbour snails, slugs and other pests if they are left to lie, but brushing out corners and cleaning behind and under pots will rid the garden of further nasties. Disentangling old growth of climbers from the supporting trellis is another outstanding job.

The garden is still suffused with scents of winter flowering shrubs – sarcococca, *Hamamelis mollis* and *Lonicera fragrantissima* all grow near to the workroom window. These shrubs should all have a place near windows so that their lovely fragrance, such a bonus in the early months, can be enjoyed.

Today I put in some work in my dark and difficult corner. At the back of the flower bed the rather splendid *Mahonia japonica* and the small-leaved bamboo, *Sinarundinaria nitida*, form a wall of shade and of course the earth underneath is very dry. In the late spring a spreading clump of *Polygonatum* (Solomon's seal), and *Smilacina racemosa* are beautiful, but as they die down the gap is depressing, and the Solomon's seal becomes a martyr to nasty grey sawfly caterpillars, which wreak unsightly havoc on the leaves. Recent browsing through books and

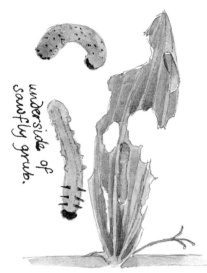

underside of sawfly grub.

Polygonatum.

particularly dry. Laurels will usually survive difficult aspects, and if the *Aucuba*, variety 'Sparkler', does well its bright variegation should dispel some of the gloom.

The spotted-leaved *Brunnera macrophylla* flourishes under shrubs and *Symphytum* 'Goldsmith' (comfrey) has a well-variegated leaf in green and pale gold, so by using these variegations this dark patch may come to life. These and the fern for dry places, plus

Symphytum 'Goldsmith' will thrive in shade.

some investigation at the Royal Horticultural Society shows produced some plants that may tolerate this situation.

I planted the common woodrush *Luzula sylvatica* 'Marginata' which the nurserywoman who sold it to me promised was absolutely foolproof for dry shade. I have seen luzulas in woodlands in Gloucestershire, certainly in shade though not apparently

Brunnera macrophylla silver spots – grows in dry shade

a few rooted pieces of the good-tempered spurge *Euphorbia robbiae*, have all been comfortably planted in well-dug soil enriched with leaf mould and some crumbled horse manure, followed by a liberal watering, and although all these plants should flourish in dry conditions they will appreciate regular watering in their first summer to give them a good start in life.

February

Looking at climbers

In my tiny garden ground space is limited but, lacking room to spread sideways, plants can always be trained to go up or down. There is a wide choice of suitable and charming climbers and trailers which with constant attention can be kept within reasonable bounds. In addition to the ivies, which make a useful backdrop on walls and fences, a good proportion of evergreens keep the garden furnished all the year round. These include two evergreen clematis. *C.armandii*, with big leathery three-lobed leaves, threatens to become rampant, but it is so handsome I am reluctant to cut it back; the sweetly scented waxen flowers are reminiscent of a Victorian nosegay and have a growth crisp and firm as a cauliflower sprig. *C.cirrhosa* var. *balearica* is less vigorous; it could in fact be said to need encouragement, but the ferny bronze leaves are delightful all the year round and the white snowdrop-like flowers with brown speckles are an early spring bonus.

As the arching wands of *Jasminum nudiflorum* lose their yellow stars, *Forsythia suspensa* 'Nymans' begins to string its pale yellow flowers along pendant sprays. Another variety growing here is *F.s.*f.*atrocaulis* which has dark purplish stems. This is very different from the brash yellow bush of the more common forsythia glaring from suburban front gardens.

An evergreen to be trained against a trellis is the dark-leaved *Osmanthus delavayi*; the leaves are tiny and leathery and the bush covers itself with sweet-smelling white flowers in March.

Trailing from pots everywhere are periwinkles – rooting wherever they can find a cranny to anchor themselves. The dark-leaved, white-flowered *Vinca minor* f.*alba* has taken longer to establish than *V.major* 'Aureovariegata' whose yellow and green leaves are particularly fresh in spring – it will flourish and flower in either sun or shade and is a natural gap-filler. Vincas need to be cut back from time to time – tidying away straggly growth and encouraging fresh shoots and bright leaves. A dark form, *Vinca minor* 'Atropurpurea', is proving hard to establish.

Forsythia
suspensa
'Nymans'

Osmanthus
delavayi

Clematis cirrhosa

Vinca major
'Aureovariegata'

Vinca minor f. alba

February

Helleborus niger and *Arum italicum* ssp. *italicum*

Hellebores are in various stages of bud and blossom all over the garden – in pots and in the bed. Reputed to be the earliest flowering is *H.niger* (*niger* referring to the root colour). I have never found this so and have certainly never achieved a Christmas display to warrant its common name of Christmas rose. I have also found it one of the most difficult to grow. Plant after plant has died away at the end of the first or second year. Things look better at present; a healthier specimen set seeds last year and young plants are popping up all over the garden. As they are likely to have chosen situations they fancy I am hoping that some will establish themselves and form strong clumps. The large white waxen flowers are beautiful and boast butter-yellow stamens; the flowers are nearer to the ground than with other hellebores and tend to get mud-splashed in wet weather. As the season progresses the flowers turn green and can be enjoyed thus for a long time.

The *Arum italicum* ssp. *italicum*, which has suffered renaming, is related to the hedgerow plant Lords-and-Ladies or Jack-in-the-pulpit. It has spectacularly veined leaves which always arrest visitors who are not familiar with the plant. The leaves appear in winter and the long arrow-head shape has a complex pattern of grey veining on dark green which is maintained for a long period. The clump I have in a large tub is steadily spreading. The flower is similar to the wayside arum, a pale green spathe with a cream spadex, which appears in spring and is rather short lived. If one is lucky and insects do a good pollinating job, a stout stem of red berries will develop and add further interest. This is a very rewarding plant, happy in a shady position and looking well with hellebores and dicentras.

Arum italicum. ssp. italicum

Hellebonus
niger

Fatsia japonica

Pyracantha
coccinea

Ilex
'Chestnut
leaved'

Aucuba
'Variegata'

February

The side garden

A large pyracantha (firethorn) entangled with *Jasminum officinale* overhangs the side garden, creating deep shade. Cut back from time to time, the canopy needs to be extensive enough to block out a nearby house, maintaining total privacy for me and the blackbird which nests cosily and rears its young in the tangled twigs. Flowering madly in June, filling the air with heavy scent, the pyracantha has nevertheless always disappointed with its meagre crop of berries. The now-substantial trunk is as gnarled and twisted as a tree depicted in a Japanese woodcut.

Apart from a patch by the front door where the early morning sun strikes and lasts long enough to allow some summer bedding to flourish, the whole area, which is below street level, is furnished with containers planted with shade-lovers. Most impressive is the *Fatsia japonica*, now over 6ft (1.8m) tall, spreading out its leathery seven-fingered leaves dramatically. It is hardy except perhaps in an exceptionally hard winter – in twenty-eight years I have lost only one, which, with more care, I think I might have nursed through the bitter weeks. Every year some leaves turn yellow and drop off, slightly alarming as this seems to indicate that death may be imminent, but new growth from the base prevents the main stem from looking naked. The flowers come in late autumn and are pollinated by a flurry of flies, leaving black berries to develop. In spring aphids may attack the developing leaf buds and, if not destroyed, will distort the new growth.

Ilex (chestnut leaf)

In pots beneath the fatsia are *Skimmia* ssp.*reevesiana* and an excellent holly bearing the label '*Ilex* (chestnut leaved)', which has large flattish mid-green leaves finely serrated that contrast well with the fatsia. The chimneypot is planted with yellow hyacinths for early flowering and these are removed when the fern which is also in the pot begins to unroll its fronds. The Japanese painted fern *Athyrium niponicum* var. *pictum* also has a home here.

For variety in this area a hydrangea will flourish for a season or two, and the low bowl has hostas, *Dicentra formosa* and white *Impatiens sultanii* (busy Lizzie) and *Begonia semperflorens* for summer months as all these tolerate the shade. I have had *Fuchsia* 'Thalia' here too. The walls are ivy-clad – an immense *Hedera algeriensis* 'Gloire de Marengo' has occupied a large pot for over twenty years and some of the variegated leaves are as large as saucers! Looking out through the sitting-room window, I am enveloped in a world of green all the year round, undisturbed by and unaware of the world beyond.

March

6 March – feeding time

The Christmas gift of a long-handled fork has been so successful that I have constructed a long-handled trowel to work alongside it. Having a number of trowels and a spare plastic vacuum-cleaner extension tube of a suitable length, I fitted (by a little whittling down of the wooden handle) the trowel firmly into the plastic tube.

plastic tube

knife for whittling

It has proved satisfactory. I find it excellent for extracting compost from the compost bin without scrabbling

compost bin

about on the ground. The compost bin takes care of all waste from the garden except the toughest prunings and evergreen clippings. It is constructed of panels that slot into one another and can be raised individually to allow compost to be taken out from the bottom while new material is still being added to the top. I find that a plastic tray positioned under the raised panel receives the scooped out compost, which can then be carried away easily to wherever it is needed, with no mess. Two boards placed across the top of the bin make a good work surface. The placing of my bin is

very unsatisfactory. To be able to remove compost from all sides it needs to be situated where there is free access all round; this one, being near a wall, is emptied only on one side and has on occasion tipped over.

The three sacks of horse manure that have been piled up all winter are now ready for spreading on the flower bed, and a handful of this rich mess can be added to pots and gently forked into the top layer together with a little compost. The manure is alive with wriggly pink worms which will probably disturb roots in the pots. I therefore introduced most of the worms to the compost bin where I hope they will do excellent work breaking down the vegetable matter. As I have few roses, one carton of fertilizer is sufficient for my needs. During the coming months it will be necessary to use a liquid feed regularly from a watering can, and an occasional foliar feed using the hose and a suitable attachment.

Although overfeeding needs to

be avoided, plants which do not receive proper nourishment will not flourish for long; when they are confined to pots or crammed together in urns, the goodness in the soil will soon be taken up. Plants that prefer poor soil will over-produce foliage on too rich a diet. Part of the interest of gardening is understanding the needs of the plants and feeding, watering and looking after their needs accordingly.

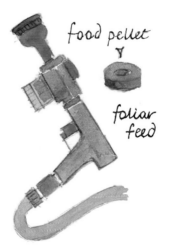

food pellet

foliar feed

20 March – window frame

The pots in the window frame (described more fully on page 73) need attention. Plants look tired after the winter and need refresher treatment; in about a month's time, when all chance of frost is past, they can go outside. The glazed doors of the frame can be opened most days to lessen the chance of mildew and moss and the plants definitely appreciate a sniff of spring air. Before repotting I go over all pots with small, very sharp scissors, trimming away all dead and dying leaves and weak growth. It is surprising how much better the plants look after this is done, and also surprising is the pile of debris that this thorough trimming produces!

I have knocked out the pelargoniums and repotted them in fresh John Innes compost with a small amount of added gravel for good drainage. Both the lotus plants, *L. maculata* and *L. jacobaeus*, have survived the winter well and I have removed a top layer of old soil and replaced it with new, adding a little compost from the bin. Fuchsias and daturas had similar treatment and all are showing healthy new sprouts.

Eucomis bulbs and begonia tubers which are stored on the top shelf can wait until next month before they are potted up and started into regrowth. The shelves below the frame are not protected by glass, but can offer some protection when the weather is really hard as a curtain of straw matting can be fixed in place for extra warmth. Here not-so-hardy subjects such as nicotianas (tobacco flowers), francoas (bridal wreath) and cuttings taken last autumn find a place.

Finally the newly potted plants are placed together and drenched with a watering can fitted with a fine rose. The frame is brushed out and the trays scoured, so that the pots can go back into a clean environment, giving the plants a good start in life.

March

A pattern of stones

A square of earth approximately 4 × 4ft (1.25 × 1.25m), which lies outside the sitting room windows in the side garden, is below a high wall and must consequently be very dry. Over the years many ideas have been tried out, but none has succeeded and as by now the huge ivy, the large jasmine and the oversize pyracantha described on page 23 all vie for rootspace, nourishment and moisture must be in short supply.

A number of granite sets became available which, together with an offer from a neighbour of a sack of large cobbles, provided enough interesting hard landscaping material to cover the area with a design of stones. To these were added some nineteenth-century ridge tiles from a builder's yard. An old sink – also never hitherto successfully planted – neatly fitted into the other shapes and, filled with rich compost, now houses two ferns,

Hedera hibernica

Polystichum falcatum 'Rochfordianum'

Polystichum falcatum

Tulipa turkestanica

T. 'Red Riding Hood'

T. Kaufmanniana

T. Turkestanica

T. 'Shakespeare'

Polystichum falcatum and the holly fern *P.falcatum* 'Rochfordianum', which should tolerate the situation provided that they are well watered. Into a small square of soil, removed and replaced by good stuff, I planted a holly, but again without success, so now an empty pot sunk into the space acts as a receptacle for different potted subjects which can be dropped into it according to season, to lodge there briefly and then be replaced. At present it holds species tulips, which have been brought on in the window frame during winter.

The stones were hammered into the soft soil, and left proud of the surface; sand and soil was sprinkled into the interstices. Rain can still permeate the gaps between the stones, and of course there is less evaporation from the soil than there was before. Strangely, the pyracantha has held its ripening berries better than in other years – has it been waiting twenty years to have stones at its feet? A very handsome pot has a central position on the granite sets, but can only be placed there on special occasions lest a light-fingered passer-by decides to make off with it, the fate of a large lemon tree which once stood in view of the road. City-dwellers have to bear in mind that garden theft is always a possibility.

Keeping the stones clean is important because their different shapes and textures can then be appreciated. Strands of ivy and jasmine must be constantly rooted out and the stones themselves regularly brushed and hosed as falling leaves lodge in the gaps.

A design of hellebores

Caring for a garden, however small, makes it difficult for the owner to go on holiday during the growing months. Even a break of two or three days entails arrangements with neighbours for watering. When much of the garden is contained in pots, however helpful and dilligent the helpers may be, the task of watering is a very individual and personal art.

Many serious gardeners take their holidays during the winter months, when there is less danger of damage through temporary neglect. So it may be now, in March, that the traveller returns from far-flung deserts or jungles, where there is either an arid waterless landscape or tropical conditions full of exotic beauties to set the gardening imagination on fire, and returns to the quiet pleasures of a northern spring. Hardly is the suitcase put down than the shutters are removed, the french windows thrown open and the inspection be-

gins. There is such pleasure in the reappearance of last year's favourites, and the leafless twigs left behind that are now sprouting fresh little buds.

At this time in March there are many hellebores: *Helleborus argutifolius*, stiff and formal with bright green flowers and architectural leaves; the graceful *H.orientalis* in many shades from white to dark purple, often prettily spotted, the easiest to grow and very profligate with its seedlings. As these do not come true from seed there are constant surprises and it is always possible that among their number will be something unusual. The group outside my workroom window is built up of three clumps. The purple *H.orientalis* is in a large pot which in summer is moved to the back of the bed; behind this, growing in the bed, is a strong *H.argutifolius*, and *H.foetidus* adds to this arrangement with smaller flowers – nodding green bells edged with maroon, leaves dark green making a finger pattern as they spread from the stem like arms outstretched. This is a variety I have had difficulty in establishing and this strong self-seeded plant chose to flourish in a tub belonging to *Rosa glauca*. Arching over this group is *Dicentra spectabilis alba* – the white form being more beautiful than the more usual pink. I grow a number of

Helleborus
argutifolius

Helleborus
orientalis

Dicentra
spectabilis
alba

Helleborus
foetidus

these in pots ready to move into positions where their outstanding grace can be fully appreciated.

Other hellebores in the garden are *H. × sternii* and the more tender *H.lividus* which needs a warm spot as its homeland is Majorca. It has decorative marbled tripartite leaves and nodding pinkish flowers and when necessary I can move its small pot complete with progeny into a position of shelter. Hellebores remain handsome for many months and their strong shapes and restrained colours

are an asset to any group of plants and shrubs with which they are associated.

Early spring flowers

Early in March some roots of primroses in pots are usually available in a local market. Dug into a few of the garden pots they flower unceasingly for several weeks, filling in gaps until the garden really wakes up. The constant succession of flowers is astonishing and it is not surprising that they are finally exhausted and there is no point in replanting them with a

view to a further show next year.

Pale yellow also is the *Epimedium perralderianum* which is one of the first epimediums to flower, sending up sprays of tiny flowers on wiry stems. White, pink and orangey-brown varieties will be coming into flower next month.

Corydalis solida – a bulbous corydalis – multiplies in a large pot below *Forsythia suspensa* and provides frail pink blooms and ferny foliage for a short period. An unusual dicentra, *D.cucullaria* also has finely cut ferny

Early spring flowers

Corydalis solida

Daphne laureola

Chaenomeles speciosa 'Nivalis'

Dicentra cucullaria

Daphne odora 'Aureo marginata'

Epimedium perralderianum

Primrose. P. vulgaris

March

foliage – the flowers, like white butterflies, spring from a glassy stem on tiny nodding stalks. Both these plants die down completely and should be marked with labels so that they are not forgotten or lost when the soil from the pots is tipped away before renewal.

The daphnes are coming into bloom – small formal bushes with leathery leaves, which grow well in pots and have a lovely scent, of which *D.odora* 'Aureomarginata' is perhaps the sweetest. This daphne has white flowers suffused with pink, while *D.laureola* and *D.albowiana* have smaller lime-green flowers which are very pretty and suit well the scheme of the pot bank where they are placed. Berries are often formed and germinate so that a little colony of seedlings clusters in the pot.

Beautiful against a dark background of evergreen foliage is one of the most choice chaenomeles, *C.speciosa* 'Nivalis' which bears chalice-shaped white flowers in clusters on its dark, angular, twiggy stems.

A few bulbs

Since the early days bulbs have not featured very seriously in the garden. In the innocent beginning, it seemed that springtime was bulb time, that a bag of daffodil bulbs could be planted in autumn and in the years ahead a carpet of yellow would cover the ground in March! This was not so – they rapidly diminished – in the third year there was one. The same happened with miniature daffodils and irises tucked into pots; they vanished. Snowdrops also disappeared year after year, but this problem was solved when I learnt about 'planting in the green'. This means obtaining the snowdrop bulbs just after they have flowered but while their leaves are still with them, rather than dry bulbs of doubtful age in cellophane packets. Sensible places such as the Royal Horticultural Society shows always have bundles of 'snowdrops in the green' at the sales areas of nurserymen who specialize in the multitudinous varieties available. Two small colonies are now establishing themselves with me, one in the bed and the other in a large tub; they are increasing every year and seem to have decided to stay.

One of the problems of bulbs in a small garden is having to wait for them to die down following the flowering period. The dying foliage is not a pretty sight, but it must be left long enough to produce nourishment for next year's bulbs, and where space is short it is inconvenient for it to be taken up with floppy, yellowing leaves. Each year any number of hyacinths are planted in pots, usually in threes and restricted to white ('L'Innocence') and pale yellow ('City of Haarlem'), both of which are touched with green in the early stages. Noble and architectural in containers, hyacinths are less suited to growing in beds and borders where they look like rather foolish sentries. They are long-lasting in flower and fill the air with delicious scent. Immediately after flowering they are removed to make room for newcomers; the old bulbs are dug in to a dark and hidden corner at the back of the flowerbed, where they take their chance, some usually surviving and coming into flower the following year with a lesser spike.

Some of the species tulips are charming and a few small pots planted with these can be briefly enjoyed and then disposed of. They are much shorter than the tulips of park bedding and they open their petals wide like small water lilies. Mostly red or yellow, with prominent yellow anthers, they make a cheerful addition among evergreen foliage, particularly the variety 'Red Riding Hood' which has leaves striped with maroon, and a potful of these is very decorative (see page 26).

Galanthus

Hyacinthus
'L'Innocence'

April

DIARY
6 April – early spring show

Today was a Royal Horticultural Society flower show day at Vincent Square, London. As you pass through the turnstile, a smell of spring pervades the air and from the top of the steps the mass of lovely displays rarely disappoints. The monthly shows are a great place to buy interesting plants seldom found in garden centres. The exhibitors' displays often show new forms and revivals of plants not much grown today, and to see so many good plants arranged together is very inspiring. There is temptation at every turn of the head, and though an impulse buy always brings pleasure it is as well to set out with ideas in mind to avoid arriving home laden with subjects for which suitable gaps are hard to find. Many of the plants for sale are quite small, which is an advantage to the gardener with a tiny patch who will have the pleasure of watching them grow to size.

By afternoon, when the coachloads from out-of-town gardening clubs have departed, festooned with purchases, and particularly at Lecture time, quiet descends and browsing is possible. There is time to ask advice of exhibitors who have plants for sale.

But where to begin, in order not to miss anything? Here are yellow aquilegias, *A.chrysantha*, a good form and long searched for, to plant in a space where white ones and a dark, almost black form already grow. *Galtonia candicans* is on my list; although some of last year's bulbs may flower again it is always worth buying some new ones to add to them. These stately summer hyacinths with tall spires of nodding white bells are a great asset in midsummer, growing in this garden to 2ft 6ins (75cm). *G.princeps* is smaller with green flowers, but is less easily available. However, a few *G.viridiflora* (a very tall form, also with green flowers) are on sale and one planted in a pot with *Euphorbia polychroma* and *Lychnis coronaria* Alba Group will look good. (The pot is positioned in full sun.) The small-leaved, bright yellow-green creeping campanula, *C.garganica* 'Dickson's Gold', is an eye-catcher. This patch of brilliance will look well under *Fuchsia magellanica* 'Alba' and *F.*'Hawkshead'. Some small rooted pieces teased away from the edge of the clump can be planted in one of the shallow pots, where, as it is evergreen, it should make a yellow cushion to brighten the winter months. The ultimate size of any plant – its height and spread – must be checked with the nurseryman; many an eight-inch charmer finishes up as an eight-foot bush, difficult to envisage at the moment of purchase and later on difficult to dig out and abandon. Years of experience have not really brought home this fact to me – it always seems it must be possible to accommodate something so desirable.

Another temptation is *Anthriscus sylvestris* 'Raven's Wing', destined to have flower heads similar to Queen Anne's Lace above frondy leaves of purple-green – but it will grow to more than four feet! Perhaps behind the *Rosa glauca* (formerly *rubrifolia*) with its glaucous pink-green leaves it could be managed? – and somehow it is in the carrier bag, having won the day.

Here is a replacement for the *Euphorbia myrsinites* that died of cold wet feet last winter – for alas, plants die away at times, from cussedness or oversight. So often overheard at monthly shows is the remark, 'You know, I used to have it, but it's gone'. Peer behind any gardener's greenhouse or compost heap and you will find the graveyard! Trying again is worthwhile, but three deaths of a kind over the years usually means that the garden, the gardener and the plant are not in harmony.

A final risky purchase: pulmonarias never 'do' in this garden, re-

sulting in death after death – mildew, shrivelled leaves, dwindling and then a sad little gap. *P.officinalis* 'Sissinghurst White' was the last to go. And now this nurserywoman is gently slipping a new pulmonaria into a plastic bag, murmuring words of wisdom and encouragement. It has large leaves with large pale spots – this is the last chance for pulmonaria.

Back home with the plants, a resolution is made to plant them soon. So often new pots are put to one side for temporary convenience and, even though they may be watered, this does not do them any good. Sometimes, however, standing them in their designated position for a short time accustoms them to the light and the neighbours before the disturbance of actual planting takes place and the nurturing, the loving care and the fulfilment begins.

DIARY
14 April – yellow

The yellow of the garden is a delight at the moment – the clear spring yellow that verges on green and is sharp and fresh without being too acid.

The favourite pot bank, which faces south, was originally planned to hide the unsightly drainpipes from the bathrooms of the flats above. Today it is a joy to look at – *Euphorbia characias*, *E.myrsinites* and *E.palustris* are all burgeoning at the front; a pale yellow broom, *Cytisus* × *praecox* 'Warminster', makes a lemon waterfall of bloom; the fresh leaves of *Lonicera nitida* 'Baggesen's Gold', the prickly bush *Berberis thunbergii* 'Aurea' and the taller golden bay are all in good shape. There is even a yellow buttercup flower on *Potentilla megalantha*. Some greys give relief from the yellow and this sunny aspect is

Laurus 'Aurea'

Cytisus × praecox 'Warminster'

Hamamelis mollis

Helichrysum italicum

Lonicera nitida 'Baggesens Gold'

E. characios ssp. Wulfenii

Berberis thunbergii 'Aurea'

Hebe pinguifolia

Euphorbia myrsinites

ideal for growing grey-leaved plants. There are very early pink buds on *Helichrysum amorginum* and the small daisy-like flowers are just opening on *Olearia stellulata*. The curry plant *Helichrysum italicum* works its way among the shrubs and a crop of very healthy grey leaves of *Lychnis coronaria* Alba Group promise plenty of white campion-like flowers in about a month's time.

At the front of this pot bank *Acanthus hirsutus* begins to grow boldly. This is its third year – an interesting acquisition from the Chelsea Physic Garden, where in their small selling area desirable and unusual plants can often be discovered.

The climbers on the trellis which hide the drainpipes include three very different clematis, the rampant (late flowering) *C.* × *jouiniana* 'Praecox', the much shyer early-flowering *C.cirrhosa* var. *balearica* and the delicate *C.*'Alba

Luxurians'; mingling with them, *Coronilla valentina* 'Citrina' and *Hippocrepis emerus* are sprinkled with yellow pea flowers. Right up the drainpipe, twining as it goes, *Akebia quinata* is reaching 20ft (6m); it is covered with three-petalled dark purple velvet flowers and is said to smell sweetly of vanilla, but soaring skyward as it is, the elusive scents are only for the pleasure of the owners of the upper windows.

20 April – self-sown seeds

Making a survey of the pots this morning, I find self-sown seedlings sprouting madly everywhere. It is intriguing to decide which they are – some are easily recognizable at the seed-leaf stage by shape and colour, for others one has to wait a little longer until the first true leaves appear. Seedlings also turn up in very unlikely places apart from the pots, spread by wind or birds – or in the case of *Euphorbia lathyris* (the caper spurge) or *Impatiens glandulifera* (Indian balsam) by the explosive nature of their seed dispersal mechanism.

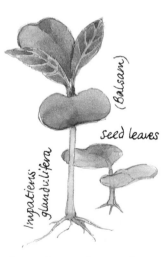

Cracks and crannies produce very healthy seedlings, the cool, non-drying root run encouraging sturdy growth. Many of them I leave to flourish in their chosen situation, as in this way edges are softened and the garden does not get that over-manicured look. Other plantlets are teased out and planted out to grow on in trays for later use.

The quantity of seedlings of specific plants in any one year is very variable. This year impatiens is prolific but *Euphorbia lathyris* is very sparse. Some years a clutch of daphne may appear, or a group of hostas, or a young clematis is found bravely clambering up a neighbouring plant. I have found progeny of my plants not only in distant neighbours' gardens but clothing paving stones in the road. Some troopers can be relied upon to reproduce themselves regularly year after year, family friends who are always welcome, like the fumitories, now rejoicing in the fancy names of *Pseudofumaria lutea* (with yellow flowers) and *P.alba* (with white flowers). These can be differentiated early as the first seed-leaves of the latter are the bluer of the two. I am watching anxiously for seedlings of the wild fumitory *P.claviculata*, which is a fragile climber.

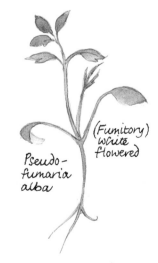

A few very prolific seeders must be weeded out – the white honesty (*Lunaria alba*) and some of the fox-

gloves (*Digitalis*) – but all the hellebore seedlings I leave, as in my experience many disappear. I collect the seeds from *H.lividus* and *H.niger*, because I find them difficult; the collected seeds are sown in pots, and two plants of *H.lividus* with well-marbled leaves are doing well.

The joy of searching for, finding and nurturing seedlings is very rewarding and enhances the feeling of continuity in the garden. It is also always a pleasure to be able to give well-grown plants to gardening friends, and who knows, my diligent probings among plants may one day produce some rare chance seedling which will bring me fame and fortune!

27 April – using plants in pots to fill spaces

I have been planting some small to medium-sized pots with subjects with which to fill the gaps left from spring pleasures when the summer arrives.

April

begonia tuber

grit

drainage crock

potting tools

hanging pot holder

meat hook

labelling

Last year's begonia corms, left to dry out over the winter, are in fairly good condition and I have bought a few more to add to them – yellow and white. Each will make a good display in quite a small pot, and the exotic, well-shaped blooms flower bravely until the autumn frosts. I no longer make the mistake of planting them upside down – a common error with new gardeners – nor do they get planted too deeply.

Eucomis bulbs, stored on the top shelf of the window frame, came in for repotting too, some had multiplied so well that they could be split up and repotted separately in rich but gritty compost. Year after year they flourish, and it is surprising that they are not grown more frequently for they are of very handsome growth and the flower spikes, with their amusing leafy tufts (hence the name 'pineapple flower'), are long-lasting and remain decorative for some time after they have gone to seed.

At this time the trays of strong-growing seedlings of nicotiana (tobacco flowers) need to be thinned out, one or two plantlets to a pot. The green and white ones, slipped into a gap in July, will immediately settle down and look at home.

Other seedlings, often self-sown, that are worth transplanting are *Pole-monium pauciflorum* (one of the Jacob's ladders), which is a smallish feathery plant with yellowy-brown flowers with a long flowering season in shade; and *Calceolaria chelidonioides*. This last is a gem – it has none of the coarseness of the over-abundant greenhouse calceolaria and the small flowers are of the clearest lemon I have ever seen. The plant is annual, but a great self-seeder, surprising one with a flash of its exquisite colour in the most unexpected places.

Twiners and fritillaries

With walls and fences to cover, climbers help to create the curtain of green that encircles and confines my small area, hiding me from others and cutting out the surrounding urban scene. Slowly over the years the climbers and wall shrubs have masked nearby buildings and railway hardware and I am now in a green enclave of my own. The climbers not only embellish the walls but in sunshine cast elegant shadows on the pale stucco of the house. Even the railway gantry becomes clad in a foam of *Fallopia baldschuanica* (mile-a-minute or Russian vine) in late summer. Pigeons use the cover at nesting time and strut up and down their own garden path, which really belongs to the railway!

Some April twiners

Clematis
montana

Clematis
macropetala

Fritillaria meleagris

LCC

Akebia quinata

April

With the days becoming lighter, the forming of buds and the first flowers are a great delight, showing that spring has really arrived. The *Clematis macropetala* literally sparkles by the front door with pale mauve-blue stars, making every return to the house joyful. It shares its trellis with *Lonicera pileata*, slow growing with tiny flowers which will develop into translucent blue berries. In their tub are other early subjects, a pale-leaved hosta, a clump of the marbled leaves of *Arum italicum* and lots of *Lunaria alba* (white honesty).

The *Clematis montana* spreads over the wooden arch which it shares with a nondescript vine. As the vine is not yet in leaf, the clematis has the arch to itself, making wreaths of pale flowers. Over the years its progeny have sprung up in very unlikely places, and a dark-leaved offspring has landed in a pot with an aged *Choisya ternata* and now rambles vaguely among all its neighbours. Tiny checked fritillaries (*Fritillaria meleagris*) reappear annually in a pot, never having flourished in tubs or the flower bed. They are very cherished, for never can a plant have been more specifically designed for an illustrator.

Euphorbias

This enormous family, commonly known as spurge, has many desirable forms for the gardener who takes pleasure in strong shapes, handsome foliage and colour varying from grey-green through bright green to green-purple. The flowers are minute and it is the showy bracts which give the display. Many forms will grow into big bushes – almost shrubs – when planted out in open beds. The earliest euphorbia, the accommodating *E.robbiae*, is looking fresh and good at present, spreading well by its creeping root stock. It grows anywhere and pieces transplanted into dry and shady spots can be relied on to do well. *E.myrsinites* pushes its glaucous-leaved stems through a retaining piece of wrought iron, its formal structure marrying well with the rusty Victorian lacework. Heads of *E.characias* ssp. *wulfenii* are opening and need to be watched for aphids. This can grow into a large and spectacular shrub but here, confined to a terra-cotta pot for many years, its size is modest and it suits the scale of the bank of pots.

Most favourite, *E.lathyris*, the caper spurge, can be found wild in the British Isles. This plant is of great architectural beauty, with its opposite, glaucous sea-green leaves and spreading bracts forming an impressive spire up to 4ft (1.2m). Strategically placed, it is guaranteed to arouse comment, and it should be better appreciated by gardeners and more frequently used. A biennial and a great self-seeder, its seeds explode from their capsules and ricochet everywhere, often sprouting in well-chosen positions, while those less fortunately placed can be easily moved and passed onto friends.

E.mellifera, now in its third year, has produced four flower heads. An enormous, statuesque plant, the leaves are well coloured and the strange, pale velvety-brown flowers seem designed to wreathe an Edwardian bonnet. In a pot it makes a striking feature, but not being reliably hardy it needs winter protection when frost persists. It smells deliciously of honey, as its name suggests.

Seedlings of *E.stricta*, the Tintern spurge, come up everywhere and are mostly left to their own devices, filling corners and later in the year providing

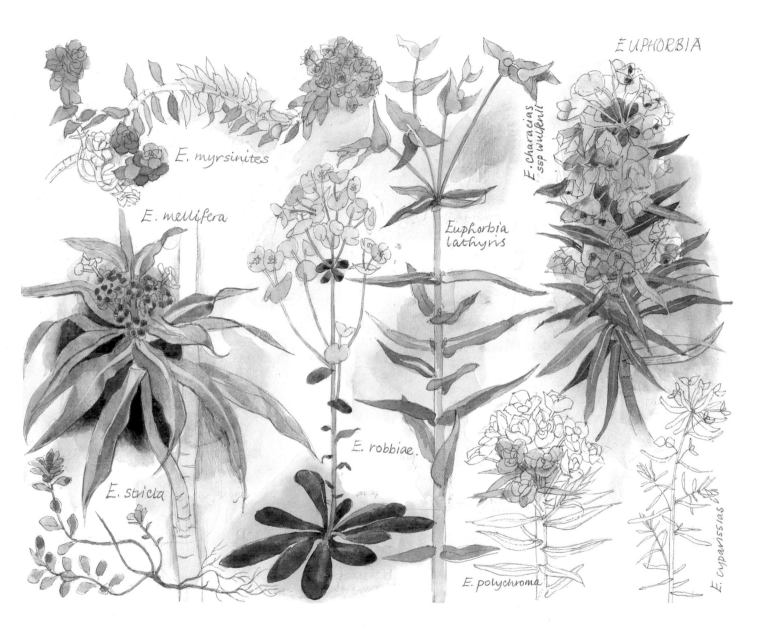

E. myrsinites

E. mellifera

E. characias ssp wulfenii

EUPHORBIA

Euphorbia lathyris

E. stricta

E. robbiae.

E. polychroma

E. cyparissias

clouds of light green confetti on pink stems, softening the outlines of pots or bursting out between stones. *E.cyparissias* is another spurge that fills areas with bright, soft, narrow leaves and yellow heads, spreading freely and linking together plants with which it is associated.

May

8 May – dealing with pests

On checking through the pots today I noticed some plants looking very sad. Tipping the contents out, I found that vine weevils have been at work. These nasty grubs nibble away at roots, separating them from the top growth which can be lifted off like a lid. The *Saxifraga* 'Haagii', a bristly plant, is cleaned and repotted and hopefully at least some sprigs will make new growth. The *Armeria* (thrift) is probably too damaged. The vine weevil is about ½in (12mm) long, has a white body and a black head; it is a scourge among plants living in pots. Saxifrages and heucheras seem to be prime targets, and these should be checked regularly. Apart from stamping on the beasts, it is necessary to discard infested soil, and even then they may persist.

Like most town gardens this one suffers badly from slugs; an energetic hunt over two weekends once pro-

vine weevils

snail

duced three hundred. Snails have never been a problem. Slug pellets have to be resorted to, but I hope that as the birds are well fed on ground-up peanuts they will avoid the pellets. (Sparrows, dunnocks, some blue tits and a robin are all feeding happily from the plastic feeders attached to the windows, and the robin arrives the minute the french windows are opened and has on occasion entered the workroom and hopped about among the papers.) Some hosta snouts are beginning to push through and I usually manage to keep them free of slugs with a sprinkling of pellets and by surrounding them with a layer of sharp grit which seems to deter the slugs. The same treatment is given to dicentras and other succulent plants. Shards of earthenware from broken flower pots, or cinders if available, will also do the trick, for slugs do not appreciate a scratchy surface.

To ensure that aphids, whitefly or other nasties are not invading plants in the window frame I have

slug

fumigated it with a smoke pellet, which should destroy lingerers from last year or new arrivals.

cone FUMIT

pellet

fumigants

16 May – garden centres

It was necessary to go to the garden centre today to stock up with John Innes Compost No. 2 (a good grade of compost for most pots), some sharp sand, which is essential for potting, and a sack of grit – used for drainage at the bottom of pots and for spreading liberally around plants prone to slug damage. I also mix grit with John Innes to form a more open and free-draining compost and find that many plants flourish in it, as the soil in pots can become clogged and sticky.

Green garden string is another important requisite for tying back plants and organizing climbers the way they should go. String, as well as being less intrusive than wire, is much less likely to damage plants or to strangle the thickening branches of shrubs. In autumn, when the deciduous plants drop their leaves, the garden is a tangled mass of green string!

There is a great difference between garden centres and nurseries. The former buy in their plants, and the latter grow them, and it is at nurseries that the more interesting and desirable plants are to be found, and where knowledgeable people are usually on hand with good advice.

Garden centres are fine for summer bedding and most true gardeners find a few bedding plants useful – although most of these can be easily grown from seed, space and time are necessary for seed boxes and potting-on processes. Also, where only one or two plants are needed a seed tray of

forty is a nuisance, and rejected seedlings sit miserably in a corner for months. The vast amount of summer bedding is for the Instant Gardener, as evidenced by the trolley loaded with costly displays of hectic colour at the check-out – everything is bright, the bright red pelargoniums, brilliant striped petunias, brilliant orange and yellow tagetes positively hurt the eyes. The summer gardener is bringing 'colour' to the garden. Many of those who have been educated to work with colour go a little wild in their gardens, regarding the flower bed as a different kind of palette, to be brightened and cheered up. Unwisely used, brilliant colour can diminish distance and draw the eye to the particular. Looking at these gardens, it appears that green in its infinite variety is not considered a colour, that whites, silvers, soft yellows and golds are invisible; only colours that shout and shriek are 'colour'. Many television programmes promote this image of the vivid garden.

Worse, almost, than this blinding array, are the 'sundries' to which garden centres devote so much floor space – the Noddy bird tables, sundials sporting shiny brass butterflies, and even, horror of horrors, imitation Victorian tricycles with plant holders soldered to them at every possible

point. How much better if the money spent on these intrusive trifles were spent on one good and beautiful pot from the hand of a true potter. So many gardens are spoilt by bright white curlicue furniture sprouting out of lawns, and features that their owners have chosen as 'original'.

DIARY
25 May

Some of the silver and grey-leaved plants make excellent space-fillers, looking equally well among dark leaves and flowers, where they prevent a group looking too heavy, or mingled with golds and yellows where they produce a scintillating paleness. I would not choose to put them among variegated plants, which usually need to be stabilized with a strong supporting colour.

The lacy *Artemisia arborescens*, whose foliage is almost white, will ramble and thread its way through its neighbours in a most engaging way. Fortunately for me it produces few flowers, as these are rather inferior yellow daisies that need to be picked off. It seems to resist drought and will survive a mild winter, but it is wise to take a few cuttings in late summer and over-winter them in a sheltered

May

Choisya ternata

Artemisia arborescens

Alchemilla mollis

Ballota pseudodictamnus

place to be sure of a supply for the following year.

Ballota pseudodictamnus is also evergreen and very hardy; it tends to get woody and leggy but responds well to being severely pruned. It also roots easily from cuttings. I grow it in several situations, but it is particularly satisfactory weaving its way through plants in the dark drift (see page 58). The leaves are pale and felty, and though the flowers are insignificant there are also tiny rosettes which are very pretty.

Another grey rambler and trailer is *Helichrysum petiolare* which needs looking after in winter and is usually regarded as summer bedding. The variety 'Limelight' is fresher in appearance. I find that helichrysum grown in pots soon flags when the compost dries out.

Alchemilla mollis grows freely in everyone's garden except mine! I see it self-seeding, springing from crevices and cracks and crannies; gardeners wail that it cannot be controlled. Every year I beg plants from those who are overrun – it condescends to endure the summer and then disappears again completely. Its beautiful pleated leaves hold dew or raindrops so that after a shower it twinkles like crystal.

No one should be without

Choisya ternata (Mexican orange) – a handsome leathery-leaved shrub, it has grown here in a pot for many years and judicious pruning has restrained its size. A bush of good growth, tolerating some shade, it produces sweetly scented waxy flowers in May. New forms are 'Sundance' with golden leaves (see page 78) and a recently introduced form 'Aztec Pearl' which has narrow, finger-like leaves. The flowers of both of these are said to be like *C.ternata*, but my plants have not yet reached the flowering stage.

Myrtus communis

The front door, May. Summer bedding and some tender shrubs

The front door

I have never considered the containers at the front door as serious gardening! Situated at the bottom of the steps leading from the street, it is important that they should be pleasing to me as I go in and out and welcoming to visitors. Fortunately, although well below street level, quite a lot of light falls here in the early morning, and an overhanging section of glass roof provides a degree of shelter in winter for some tender shrubs in pots. This group is primarily a summer feature; there are two troughs with pots in front, and hanging baskets, and the window sill adds an extra level. *Pseudofumaria alba* and an acanthus have seeded themselves in the troughs and the former keeps its leaves in winter, providing some green-ness together with added pots of ivy.

In May the soil in the troughs is replaced and a selection of the less aggressive bedding plants is put in. Being an annual event, the scheme can be varied; a pink and white year was prettily effective, with delicate pink ivy-leaved pelargoniums, shell pink *Begonia semperflorens*, white impatiens and trailing lobelia. A month or so later I added white, sweet-smelling nicotiana (tobacco flowers). A brown and silver year was more unusual –

43

the dark maroon leaves of *Begonia semperflorens* with white flowers, white impatiens, *Oxalis triangularis*, *Aeonium arboreum* 'Atropurpureum' interwoven with *Ballota pseudodictamnus* and *Helichrysum petiolare*. Later some of the darkest nicotiana gave more height.

The plants need spraying with water regularly as the dust from the road blows in; they also need to be sprayed occasionally with an insecticide because this location is particularly prone to red spider and whitefly which despoil the leaves – both are difficult to control. As pesticides harm beneficial insects as well as pests, the use of biological controls is always a preferable and sounder option.

Pots come and go – an orange tree in its pot hibernates under the shelter of the glass roof and three small myrtles – *Myrtus communis*, *M.communis* 'Variegata', and *M.communis* 'Jenny Reitenbach' – are at home there at present and give off a pleasing smell when a leaf is crushed.

A butt catches rainwater from the roof and in a pot on top of it, kept very wet, is the grass *Miscanthus sinensis* 'Variegatus'. Under the shelf that supports the butt is a protected spot where pots containing non-hardy subjects can be tucked away in winter and given extra cover if necessary.

Trailers

In a garden of many levels, trailers, whether evergreen or deciduous, are of great value throughout the year – dropping from pots fixed to walls, from pots in jardinières and pot-stands, they will add a curtain of green. Where there is a flight of steps, trailers will tumble down them from a well-placed pot. The little ivy-leaved toadflax, *Cymbalaria muralis*, is everywhere, the mauve form common on old walls, or the rarer white form 'Nana Alba' which obligingly grows quite easily from seed. *Asarina procumbens* has been with me for many years, and here it is quite hardy – it does not seem very fussy about its flowering season, and this can be prolonged by nipping off the seed capsules, which are very prolific. *Antirrhinum hispanicum*, with a similar snapdragon-type flower in palest pink, trails its grey woolly leaves by the yard and also is a great seed producer – as it is only its first year I have yet to discover how viable these seeds are, and whether next year there will be a glut of little plants.

Two summer trailers are *Lotus maculatus* and *L.jacobaeus*. Both of these have pea-like flowers and in no way resemble the lotus flower of common parlance. The flowers of *L.jacobaeus* (see page 60) are dark chocolate with a dash of gold and look exactly like a swarm of bees. *L.maculatus* has finer and greyer foliage and covers itself in yellow lobster claws. Both should be given a position where they can be appreciated.

Trailing nasturtiums in the right position will tumble out of pots and the peltate leaf shapes are a useful design element. Careful selection of colour is necessary and for this garden a creamy yellow form has been very successful; there is also a variety with a variegated leaf, which needs to be carefully placed or it looks busy, and a dark-leaved one with deep red flowers which is handsome.

Jasminum parkeri is a yellow-flowered jasmine that will hang from a pot, and the growth is small and neat; it flowers from early May to June. Quite a number of fuchsias are the weeping type, but having a personal horror of some of the large-flowered overblown varieties I look for those with smaller, neater flowers. A small box of trailing lobelia will provide enough plants to tuck into the edges of containers for summer flowering. When winter comes along there is a vast variety of ivies to choose from, to fill in gaps left after deciduous subjects have faded.

Using height

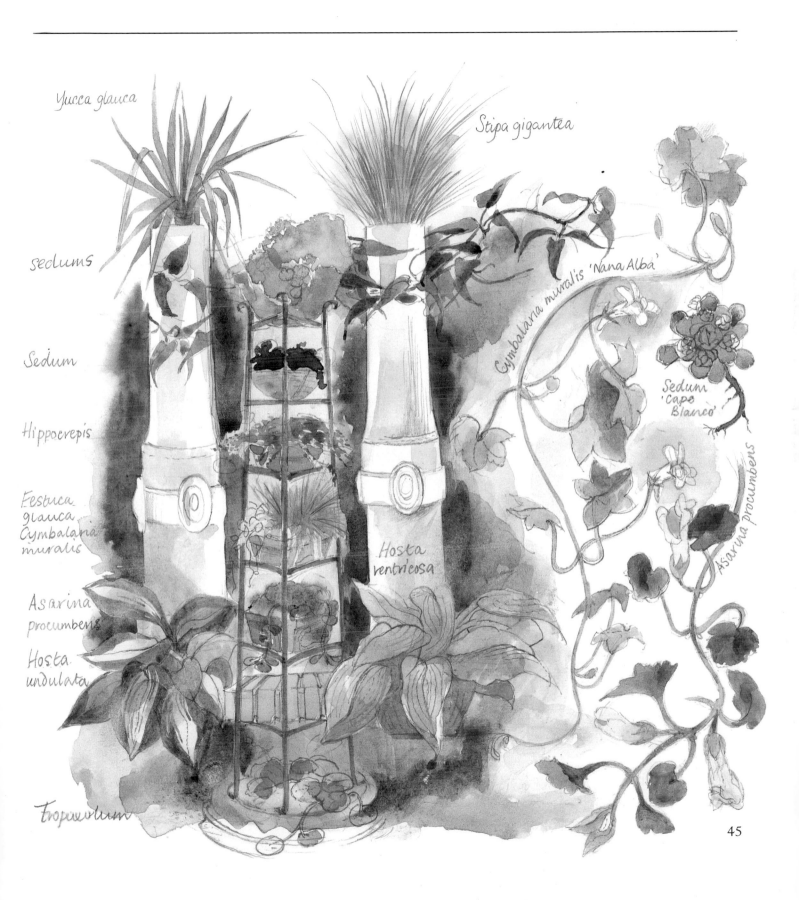

Yucca glauca

Stipa gigantea

sedums

Cymbalaria muralis 'Nana Alba'

Sedum

Sedum
'Cape
Blanco'

Hippocrepis

Festuca
glauca
Cymbalaria
muralis

Asarina procumbens

Hosta
ventricosa

Asarina
procumbens

Hosta
undulata

Tropaeolum

45

May

Hostas

In the last few years the hosta has become high fashion; at plant sales there are displays showing great variety and several books devoted to it are now available. It is a splendid plant and deserves its popularity, but needs to be kept clean and fresh and above all free from snails and slugs which, by the end of the summer, will have turned most of the handsome leaves to tatty lace if not controlled.

The hostas here are *not* eaten; on Open Days this causes a great deal of comment – about fifteen varieties, all flourishing uneaten! Snails have never been a problem in this garden, and to combat the large number of slugs, slug pellets are used, and used early, before the succulent hosta snouts push through the soil – but I believe the success is mainly due to the thick layer of sharp grit with which I surround each plant, whether in a pot or in the ground, and which

Hosta sieboldiana var elegans.

June

from time to time is topped up when the layer has become scattered by watering. Moreover, the hostas here flourish amazingly and I can only think that the garden now provides a microclimate to which they are particularly suited. It was not always so – in the early years I lost several plants and temporarily gave them up; but the garden climate has probably changed as it has become increasingly full of plants, and it may be that the gardener has also changed and become better at her job!

The choice of hosta varieties is confusing and to the untutored eye many of them look very alike. *H. tarda* is a particular favourite; stuffed into a pot in full sun it does well but, being confined, its leaves are small, which suits its position. There are two or three plants with yellow and green variegation which are lovely in spring but turn a dull green as the months progress. Others retain their variegation well and 'Zounds' holds its butter yellow throughout. A handsome *H. erromena* in an urn almost vies with *H. sieboldiana* for the size of its leaves. All flower well, but the spikes are mostly of a washed-out mauve and die untidily. It is those marvellous leaves which make the display and give so much decorative form wherever there is room to place them.

DIARY
5 June – acquiring plants

Now is the time to tuck a few extra plants into containers and the jardinière. The acquiring of plants is a great pleasure, and the sight of rows of them waiting to be taken home and nurtured fills one with desire! Looking carefully before buying will help to avoid disappointment as well as wasted money, for there are quite a lot of traps for the unwary. Reliable nurseries or plant stalls at the Royal Horticultural Society's shows will usually be offering healthy, well-grown plants – but not always. Many garden centres are careless about looking after the plants they buy in for resale, particularly with regard to watering or attack by pests. Street markets need a careful eye – much of what they are selling is the surplus from growers and nurseries and will be suffering from old age and rough handling, although looking carefully among these it is sometimes possible to pick up bargains. Wherever plants are bought, they should be checked over to see that they are free from disease, aphids or worse, which could be introduced into the garden.

If a lot of roots protrude from the container, then the plant is probably potbound; it may be possible to dis-

entangle roots wound tightly round one another and to plant them so that the roots sit comfortably in sifted compost in their new position, but even then the plant may have been too disturbed to flourish. Removed from the container and simply planted as it is, there is faint hope of it establishing itself. Plants in nurseries may have thrust their roots into the soil on which the container is standing, so disturbance may cause a setback; it may be difficult to ease the plant from the container without damage, even by cutting the pot away with a sharp knife. The aim is to find a healthy plant, with good, firm green leaves, not in full flower, but with evidence of flowers to come – and with roots still in the container. A gentle tug will ensure that the plant actually has some roots! The plant should be labelled or the nurseryman persuaded to label it.

June

Back in the garden, pots are set in a shady place and well watered (both foliage and compost) and given time to get over the journey – like people, they appreciate a little consideration!

DIARY
15 June

The umbrella leaves of *Darmera peltata* (which used to be called *Peltiphyllum peltatum*) are growing to a good size – they make an impressive clump at the edge of one of the pot banks where I need strong shapes. Bright yellow-green in the early part of the year, by late July they achieve a crumpled russet, mixing well with the 'dark drift' to which they are adjacent (see page 58).

Being a bog plant, darmera needs the soil to be constantly damp and I have overcome this problem by sinking the pot in a plastic kitchen bowl concealed by large washed pebbles. For the rest of the summer the water must be regularly topped up to counter evaporation and the plant's thirst. On top of the darmera's pot is another moisture-lover, *Carex petriei* (a type of sedge), which sucks up some of the water itself and keeps down evaporation from the darmera's

soil. Both plants appear very happy and there are pretty flower heads among the grass blades. Another nearby plant that needs regular watering is *Lobelia* 'Queen Victoria'. The grass and the lobelia's colours fit well with the surrounding dark plants.

Flowers in June

Many of the June flowers are pale with a pretty, frail beauty that brings to mind the meadows of the past, when a child could gather handfuls of cuckoo flowers, milkmaids, and moon daisies with no thought of extinction or conservation. Not so long ago I saw, while wandering on a Mongolian hillside, the summer flowers of our gardens growing in wild

profusion – campanulas, delphiniums, dianthus, daisies, gentians and many others starred the long grass as far as the eye could see. How right they looked mingled together, not set in the clumps beloved of so many gardeners. I hope that, in a small way, the early summer flowers growing in my flowerbed have this casual quality.

As there is room for so few they must be well chosen. The aquilegias (Granny's bonnets) I grow are white, both single and double, and a lovely airy yellow – *A.chrysantha* – as well as a stunning black. As aquilegias are notorious for cross-fertilizing it is satisfactory that the black one has gone to seed before the yellow one is in flower, so hopefully the yellows will multiply next year. These plants tend to be short-lived but they usually provide plenty of seedlings.

Different varieties of the campanula (bellflower) family cover the summer months. Presently *C.alliariifolia* and *C.persicifolia* are pretty among the aquilegias and below them two of the more common fumitories are a mass of ferny leaves and delicate flowers. These two were called *Corydalis*, but are now *Pseudofumaria lutea* (yellow) and *P.alba* (white) – both so charming that they cannot be too prolific. Other desirable members of

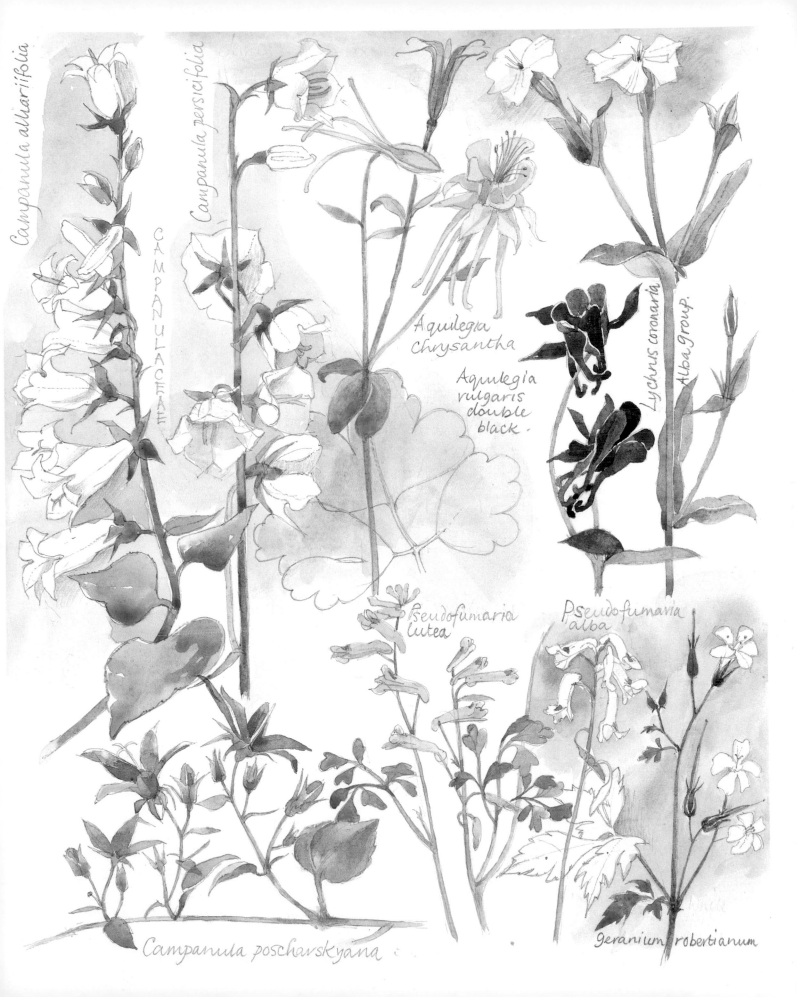

Campanula alliariifolia

Campanula persicifolia

CAMPANULACEAE

Aquilegia
Chrysantha

Aquilegia
vulgaris
double
black.

Lychnis coronaria Alba Group.

Pseudofumaria
lutea

Pseudofumaria
alba

Campanula poscharskyana

Geranium robertianum

Rosa canina

Convolvulus
cneorum

Astrantia
helleborifolia

Astrantia
major

Geranium
phaeum

June

the corydalis family which are not so fecund are tucked into pots – *C.solida*, a bulbous subject, with pinky-mauve flowers which disappears completely in early summer, *C.wilsonii*, pale yellow with the bluest leaves, and *C.cheilanthifolia*, another yellow with leaves tending to bronze.

Flowering at present in every available cranny is the mauve *Campanula poscharskyana* (creeping bell-flower) and a newly acquired white-flowered Herb Robert is rapidly taking up residence in a similar way.

A very favourite plant is *Lychnis coronaria* Alba Group (white rose campion). Long lasting and of striking angular growth, its felty grey leaves and simple flowers are very satisfying. Its brightly coloured relatives lack the style of the white form.

Garden visitors

Some visitors came by appointment this evening, a good time to look at this garden for the transverse light gives depth and emphasizes form that is not apparent during the middle of the day and the early afternoon. Garden visitors may come on Open Day, or they may telephone and come by appointment. Information about gardens open to the public is circulated by garden societies and in the local and national press, and full details of all gardens throughout England and Wales that have Open Days organized by the National Gardens Scheme are published in its annual 'Yellow Book', which is widely available from book-sellers. Clutching this guide visitors make long pilgrimages to see gardens even as small as mine. Whether the visitors come alone or on Open Day, there is time to talk and exchange experiences, and as we talk I see the garden through their eyes – a new view! (In such a small space it is preferable not to have too many visitors at once.)

Many visitors are owners of, or about to own, small gardens, so there is a pleasant smattering of young people who are looking for ideas and answers to their problems. Some come for the charming reason that they just like small town gardens. All are astonished at the number of plants growing happily in this tiny space, and appreciate the controlled design where it would be easy to arrive at a happy muddle; interest is shown in the way fairly rampant climbers are trained to fit the space, for example *Clematis × jouiniana* 'Praecox', *C.armandii*, and the rose 'Félicité et Perpétue'. The variety of leaf shapes is a source of interest, and the number of plants closely planted in two urns and doing well causes comment until they remember the way wild flowers are crammed together in hedgerows and even on motorway verges. I am humbled by their interest and enthusiasm and knowledge.

There are visitors from overseas – French, Dutch, and a couple of Americans visiting gardens in Europe who wish to see one or two modest English gardens. This patch 24 × 18ft (7.75 × 5.5m) must have been quite a contrast to Blenheim, where they had been the day before; but there was much camera clicking, so this small garden may take its appropriate place when lectures are given to gardening clubs back home.

At other times there are professional visitors, nurserymen, writers, photographers. The latter arrive with their complicated equipment, even with girls to support them on the tops

June

of ladders for the aerial view; they come in the evening to catch the slanting sunshine, or at six-thirty in the morning for the soft early light; they kneel, and bend and peer and adjust their lenses, and one is amused and flattered that such a little patch is worthy of their enthusiasm!

Visiting other people's gardens

I also enjoy visiting other people's gardens in my neighbourhood to find new ideas and inspiration. In large towns many surprises are hidden away. To discover a number of beautiful and well-considered gardens in an area of no more than two square miles proves the enthusiasm of the city-dweller for growing things and creating an oasis in a hostile environment. All these gardens are very different, reflecting both the personality of the gardener and the amount and quality of his or her private space.

Many gardeners in Britain open their gardens once or twice during the summer months under the National Gardens scheme to share their enthusiasm and pleasure with others. The proceeds from the modest entry charge go to charity. Many devoted district organizers of the scheme plan each season, checking and selecting gardens large and small that have

sufficient interest to make a visit worthwhile for visitors who may have come a long way and who should be rewarded with a range of plants and a high standard of garden design. Teas or plants for sale are added attractions, certain to draw the crowds!

From the point of view of the owner, there is much preparation – a good watering the night before to refresh the leaves and a very thorough brushing of paths and steps makes an amazing amount of difference, plus last-minute dead-heading and the removal of faded leaves. Posters and signposts must be in place and, just before the appointed time, a table is set out with leaflets, change and tickets, with a smiling helper to take the money and welcome visitors. Most of those who visit the smaller gardens are eager to talk to the owner, to find out and write down the names of plants and discuss cultivation problems and ideas.

A beautiful, long narrow garden in this part of London holds a wealth of lovely plants; the plant associations are carefully planned, shapes and masses are deeply considered. Only the best varieties of plants are there, and they are mostly plants that flourish in shade, the exquisite *Saxifraga cuscutiformis*, the not-quite-hardy *Francoa ramosa*, some lovely ferns in-

cluding the Japanese 'painted fern'. This garden is also distinguished by the most beautiful garden pots of a dark aubergine to bronze colour, completely in accord with the tranquil design, planted with *Heuchera* 'Pewter Moon', *H.micrantha* 'Palace Purple' and with the glaucous-leaved *Hosta* 'Halcyon'. They provide an arresting display as the visitor follows the thread of the garden through one area to the next until coming to rest on the long bench that spans the end wall under the fragrant 'Guinée' rose, enjoying the cross light at the end of the day when most of the visitors have gone.

Less than ten minutes away, in an unlikely setting on a steeply sloping site, the owner has created a garden of big leaves. This carefully designed pattern of foliage is deeply enclosed and has a quality of mystery. Flowers are not important and light dapples through the great leaves onto an underplanting of ferns, hostas and hellebores and other interesting shade-lovers. In this garden one moves upwards; a rising path interspaced with steps leads to the top where there is a small forest pond and one can stand, looking downwards, having an unusual aerial view of many of the subjects from above.

Again on sloping ground, a very

Visiting other people's gardens

different and much larger garden has been created from part of an old estate. Here there are fine tall trees, which have been incorporated into the design. The front of the handsome early-nineteenth-century house has a *Clematis viticella* and roses climbing its white façade to 30ft (9m), breathtakingly beautiful. On the paved terrace in front, many self-seeded plants such as lavenders and alchemilla tumble over the stones. Spires of lilies, *Acanthus spinosus*, paperwhite hollyhocks, *Nepeta govaniana* and other handsome herbaceous plants abound, and through a simple arch in a great beech hedge one begins a descent of winding paths where one delight unfolds to reveal another and there is a sound of running water and a murmuring of bees.

Arisaema consanguineum

Anisaema
speciosum

Arum
Zantedeschia aethiopica

In the window frame, June to July

At the time of year when the window frame is emptied of the over-wintered tender subjects, which are now out in the garden, it is worth using the space to grow a few unusual plants in pots. These can be varied from year to year. The genus *Arisaema* includes some that are fascinating and dramatic both in colour and shape; the shapely spathes have a spadix which may be as much as fifteen inches long. Allowed to die down slowly, the bulbs may be dried off and saved for another year. Some of them are very costly, but the less affluent gardener should be able to find enough choice from among the more modestly priced varieties.

Arisaema candidissimum.

Arisaema tortuosum.

Yucca

Puya
Mirabilis

Euphorbia
lathyris

Clematis x
Jouiniana
'Praecox'

Milium
effusum
'Aureum'

Zantedeschia
aethiopica

Pelargonium 'L'Élégante'

Hedera helix 'Ivalace'

Gazania

From the workroom window, June

July

The hours of sunshine through these long summer days mean much more attention must be paid to watering. Having so many plants in pots sometimes makes this burdensome, but careful and fairly individual watering of pots focuses the attention on the development and needs of the plants – pest infestation, mildew and other horrors are less easily overlooked when regular watering is in progress. Even heavy rain does not always permeate pots, nor does swishing a hose hither and thither or turning on a sprinkler, activities which may temporarily freshen but do not really provide plants with the moisture they need. With the hose and a suitable attachment, foliar feeding is possible, and for smaller pots liquid feed added to a watering can will keep them flowering freely. A high-nitrogen food will promote healthy leaf growth whereas potash encourages flowering. Outlay on fertilizers is money well spent, for it is wasteful to buy good plants and then let them dwindle away from starvation.

Another high-summer duty at the moment is constant dead-heading. Like the pot-watering this helps one to keep a check on the welfare of plants and it encourages repeat flowerers to keep going throughout the summer months. Annuals which are not dead-headed and are allowed to go to seed will very soon cease flowering – having produced seed, they feel that their job is done. It is worth leaving a few seed heads for propagation next year or where some self-seeding is desirable.

Dead-heading needs to be neatly done. The removal of a flower head from the top of the stalk is unsightly; both the head and the stem should be removed, and at the same time dead and dying leaves can be trimmed away. By this kind of careful attention the appearance of the garden is much enhanced.

The garden is at present very flowery and in the evening it is sweetly scented by the jasmine blossom,

which will continue to embroider the perimeter for some time to come. I have rooted cuttings of the pink-flowered *Jasminum × stephanense* which I hope will be flowering by next year. A very free-flowering hydrangea that has been living in the same pot for many years continues to perform well; I believe this to be because it is severely pruned and very well fed. In the bed are several astrantias (masterwort or melancholy gentleman); all are delicate but the bright pink *A. maxima* enchants all who come to the garden.

A pale yellow yarrow, *Achillea* 'Moonshine', was originally chosen to inhabit a small urn. As achilleas withstand poor weather so well it is surprising that they are not more often found displayed in pots, and now a good rooted piece planted in

July

the bed is spreading pale yellow plate-like heads among the strong fresh growth of *Helleborus argutifolius*.

There are more flower spikes than ever before on the hostas. Grown here for their foliage, this year's blooming is nevertheless very acceptable. The leaves of my slug-free hostas are a source of great pride to me and amazement to others.

Everywhere tufts of *Milium effusum* 'Aureum' (Bowles' golden grass), *Euphorbia stricta* with clouds of green, and *Pseudofumaria*, a mass of ferny fronds and delicate flowers, fill any available gaps.

Rearranging the 'dark drift'

Moving the pots about to make satisfying shapes and colours is a designer's pleasure and also one of the advantages of having mobile plants of various sizes with which to make new schemes. Although many different kinds of plant – climbers, shrubs and herbaceous – grow here in pots, this is not to be thought of as a 'container garden', which suggests arrangements of formality, rigidity and neat alignment. Here the pots are gathered together, mounted and arranged to form 'banks' of different heights and shapes that are planned to comple-ment one another in colour, texture and form.

The 'dark drift' is an area of dark-leaved plants that thread their way through a group of pots leading to a backdrop of spiky *Berberis thunbergii* 'Rose Glow' and a bronze-leaved *Hydrangea serrata* 'Preziosa', which has early flowerheads of limey-bronze that turn to a stunning pink – a surprising accent in this garden of muted colour. The brown flowers of *Verbascum elegantissimum* 'Helen Johnson' look delicious in this context. Two heucheras, the brown *H. micrantha* 'Palace Purple' and a newer and very desirable introduction, 'Pewter Moon', whose leaves have a silver sheen veined with dark green and backed with claret, are the base plants; above them massed together in a bowl are the dark purple leaves of *Oxalis triangularis* (not hardy, this winters in the window frame and spreads with a tuberous root stock). *Lobelia* 'Queen Victoria' provides strong vertical leaves and has brilliant red flowers and the dark-leaved *Eucomis comosa* provides a dramatic accent, and among these *Cordyline australis* spreads out its brown leaves.

A fibrous-rooted *Begonia semperflorens* with glossy brown leaves and white flowers will flourish until the winter frosts with the minimum of attention. Growing strongly after a struggle is an aeonium; this broken runt from a bargain box outside a local florist threatened to die several times, until, taking drastic measures, I cut off its feeble roots and repotted it in good gritty compost. Now a good plant, it needs to be treated like a tender succulent and kept dry during the winter months. The frothy bronze fennel, *Foeniculum vulgare* 'Smokey', contrasts well with the strong leaf shapes of the other plants.

Among other dark-leaved plants that sometimes take a place in the 'dark drift' are the easily grown black grass *Ophiopogon planiscapus* 'Nigrescens' and a little trailing bush, *Euonymus nanus* var. *turkestanicus*, which retains its leaves throughout the year and although the fresh ones are green they turn a mahogany colour in autumn and winter. There is also a place for the sage, *Salvia officinalis* Purpurascens Group.

Anthriscus sylvestris 'Raven's Wing', an umbellifer with dark feathery leaves, has to grow in the bed on account of its size, alongside *Rosa glauca*; the combination of pinky-brown and grey is very satisfying.

Eucomis
comosa

Darmera
peltata

Heuchera micrantha
'Palace Purple'

Oxalis
triangularis

Aeonium
arboreum
'Atropurpureum'

Clematis
viticella

Berberis
thunbergii
'Rose Glow'

Sedum
'Vera Jameson'

Heuchera
'Pewter Moon'

Lotus
jacobaeus

July

A choice of dark plants

Where the colour range in a garden scheme is limited, as in a small area such as mine where too many colours together can become confusing, variety can be introduced by using dark plants to give richness and depth. Mixed with grey and silver-leaved plants, interesting patterns can be created. Patient searching will reveal all manner of shapes, heights and textures with which to experiment.

Two very dark purple-flowered clematis are useful, *C. × jackmanii* and *C. viticella* – I prefer the latter because of the acute angle at which the flowers grow from their black wire-like stems, and my plant, a last year's seedling, is already flowering cheerfully. A dark berberis – *B. thunbergii atropurpurea* – has rich brown leaves, and another variety I grow, called 'Rose Glow', is flecked with pink if grown in a good light.

Aeonium arboreum 'Atropurpureum' is fleshy and mahogany-coloured and makes a good contrast both in texture and shape. Again it needs a good light, and the rosettes will achieve an impressive size, as in the garden of Barnsley House in Gloucestershire, though it will be some years before mine becomes such a fine specimen.

There are several dark sedums, from browny-pink to deepest purple, useful for hanging over edges or for growing at a low level, and all are very hardy and are loved by bees. *Lotus jacobaeus*, tender but well worth looking after, has pea-like flowers the size and colour of bumble bees even to a touch of gold, and they flutter and hover in the slightest breeze. For summer use, several varieties of *Begonia rex* have fine dark leaves; and two basils, *Ocimum basilicum* 'Dark Opal' and 'Purple Ruffles', have leaves that are almost black. A great black spire to rise above everything else is the hollyhock *Alcea rosea* 'Nigra'.

July

Endearing thugs

Some plants are very free with their favours! Although one may love them, too many can become a nuisance and hard-hearted uprooting must be undertaken.

The greatest garden thug of all was firmly established in my patch of mud when I arrived – probably a survivor from the previous Victorian garden of which mine is a morsel, or from the adjoining railway bank where it still flourishes. This is *Polygonum cuspidatum* (now renamed *Fallopia japonica*), such a determined intruder that it seems able to force its way through concrete. It must be torn out ruthlessly wherever it appears – and after twenty-eight years it still rears its awesome head. It is actually a very handsome plant and a good stand of it where space permits is impressive.

Another polygonum, *P.baldschuanicum* (now *Fallopia baldschuanica*), I introduced myself in my ignorant early days to cover a bare fence. It has been covering everything ever since; it also mounts a railway girder (where two pigeons choose to nest) before it sets off across the railway line to the embarrassment of passing trains. Though rooted out and cut back with shears, it is incorrigible and will outlive me; even so its foam of white flowers in July and August is lovely.

The Indian balsam, *Impatiens glandulifera*, is a riverside plant and very shallow-rooted, wilting quickly on a warm day. Though invasive it is easily pulled out; but it is useful and effective in July and August when sometimes there is a dearth of plants in flower. The houttuynia most commonly seen is 'Chameleon', a form with a variegated leaf that I find particularly nasty. The one in this garden is *H.cordata* 'Flore Pleno'; although it spreads alarmingly by underground stems, popping up everywhere, the leaf is handsome with a metallic sheen and the white, cone-shaped flowers mingle happily with everything. There is a smell of orange peel about it and it is said that the leaves can be used in salad.

The starry summer jasmine, *Jasminum officinale* (the old country name is Jessamine) fills the garden with its perfume on summer evenings. It is a good city-dweller and a great joy; it is also a great space invader, but in this case it is allowed to have its way. Other summer-flowering jasmines – *J.polyanthum*, which needs a protected sunny wall, and the pink-flowered *J. × stephanense* – are less prolific.

Balsam - Impatiens
glandulifera

"Jessamine
Jasminum
officinale

Houttuynia cordata
'Flore Pleno'

July

White in the garden: the jardinière

Originally used primarily in conservatories, the old Victorian jardinières are still charming pieces of garden furniture whether used indoors or out. They may still be obtained, at a price, at garden antique sales and some lucky gardeners may have inherited one from an ancient horticultural aunt. This one, a modern reproduction, was a retirement present and after ten years in the garden looks as though it had grown there – no longer bright and white and wiry, shouting 'look at me!' but now generously filled with plants, some ordinary, some more rare and needing to be cossetted. Not only is it a point of interest at all times, but when the garden has an in-between period the burgeoning and blooming jardinière helps to bridge the gap. This particular jardinière holds about twenty pots, which have to be watched because they dry out quickly and need daily watering and plenteous feeding.

At present it is enjoying a white flowering and a garden designer, visiting the other day, was particularly complimentary, admiring especially the variety of whites making up the arrangement. White gardens, she said, were usually bleak in their whiteness, but she found the present choice of whites – cream, blue-tinted, pinkish, leaning to mauve – achieved

Fleshy leaves
stem rooting

Lobelia erinus.

Sempervivella
(Rosularia sedoides)

depth and vibrance by their juxtaposition.

Ever since the White Garden at Sissinghurst was created by Vita Sackville-West, there have been admirers and imitators in every kind of garden, great and small. Although my garden uses a lot of white-flowered plants it has never been planned as wholly white. What has happened in and around the jardinière was accidental, although it may have been intuitive. In the past I have created costumes and fabric pictures making use of the depth and textures of a variety of whites, and in this arrangement of plants I have followed the same principal.

The pelargoniums (florists' geraniums) – the single white and the crisp, ivy-leaved *P.*'L'Elegante' blushed with pinky-mauve – are now blooming freely after their winter sojourn in the window frame. Some gazanias (also winter-protected), bought as a market-stall bargain last year, are also doing well. Gazanias can be very strident in colour but these are pale yellow to cream with the distinctive bird's-eye markings; the grey-green leaves are thick and felty and very good to look at. A very white impatiens flowers endlessly, throwing out glassy stems at weird angles.

Three small-flowered subjects –

a trailing lobelia whose white flowers show shreds of blue; *Sempervivella*, a charming alpine with the wax-textured flowers of a Victorian bridal wreath, now called *Rosularia sedoides* var.*alba*; and an unidentified sedum which verges to brown – are all very textural.

The highest pot-holder of the jardinière is crowned with *Eucomis autumnalis*, whose distinctive leaves are crisply arched with curly edges; three spikes of greenish-white pineapple flowers look exotic.

The jardinière is backed by a very beautiful but unidenti-fied lace-cap hydrangea which is suffused with the palest pink, and behind this rises *Hebe salicifolia*, shooting off a myriad flowers like fireworks, white with a tinge of purple anthers.

The jardinière in July

Eucomis autumnalis

Sempervivella

Pelargonium 'L'Élégante'

Lobelia erinus

sedum

Antirrhinum hispanicum

Hosta fortunei 'Aureomarginata'

65

August

2 August – notebooks

Keeping my plant notebook up to date is important and, as today, I like to check the flowering times of different subjects, adding each plant as its flowers open and noting the reappearance of subjects where top growth completely disappears in winter. The difference in flowering times is interesting – some plants flower on exactly the same date every year, others vary by as much as a month, suggesting that some are more influenced by weather conditions than others, some are purely erratic. Should I really have my *Vestia foetida* covered in green bells in March? Why does the supposedly late-flowering *Cestrum parqui* appear in April? – it is supposed to give off its delicate perfume at ten o'clock at night, but not of course on a chilly early spring evening.

A distressing aspect of this notebook is the record of plants that have flowered here and are no more, but all gardeners have to come to terms with some losses.

Another notebook accompanies me to shows to record lists of desirables at present unavailable, or to gardens for notes on plants I admire; some remain on a waiting list for a long time, others are acquired from friends, as gifts of cuttings or seedlings. This is a lovely way to add to one's garden, for happy memories of friends become woven into the tapestry.

In a larger garden planning notes may also be a help – but in as small a space as this the eye and memory usually suffice.

DIARY
25 August

Plants are beginning to grow too *big* and, as usual at this time of year, I feel a little threatened that I shall be overtaken, even engulfed, and that – like the Triffids – plants will begin to push their way through the workroom windows. Some snipping with a pair of secateurs or clippers will tidy hearty growers into better shape. For instance, the *Hebe salicifolia*, its display of white fireworks over, spreads in all directions and although the seedheads are charming and could remain in a larger garden, here, I am afraid,

the executioner must get to work. The golden privet also leans out with too-long golden wands and *Clematis × jouiniana* 'Praecox', still flowering, wanders ruthlessly across anything in its path. Judicious snipping of lengthy strands and dead flower sprays will keep it within bounds until it is properly cut back next month. This clematis must now be twenty years old; it has constantly delighted with its mauve-grey flowers and is much admired by visitors to the garden to whom I always recommend it.

The flower spikes on the June and July hostas are beginning to look rather sad; somehow the washed-out mauve is reminiscent of fading funeral wreaths. With flower spikes removed, the leaves of the hosta plants will remain impressive for two more months. The flower spikes that have been fertilized by bees and have swelling seed pods are worth leaving on the plant until ripe. Sown when fresh, the seeds should germinate next spring and if gradually potted on will make sizeable plants in three years. In a garden where both hostas and bees are numerous, cross fertilization may take place with interesting results.

Plants in pots still need a periodic liquid feed to keep them flowering for at least another six weeks.

The climbing *Dicentra macrocapnos* in its third year is now established in a pot – its frail tendrils and pale green glaucus leaves stretch across the trellis on the sunny wall, covering it with

trusses of pale yellow purse-like flowers. It is a beauty! In winter it dies back completely and the crown is then covered with leaves and dry fern fronds held in place by nylon mesh to protect it from frost. It is a plant of such delicate and unusual beauty that it merits all possible care and attention.

View with *Rosa glauca*

Roses have never occupied a very important place in this garden. In the early unknowledgeable days, when I was still believing those who told me that nothing would grow in my impoverished soil under the dripping lime trees, I chose subjects that I saw growing successfully nearby. Over the

fence were 'Superstar' roses, so I bought two standards and they did well. Later I added 'Gail Borden' and 'White Swan', hybrid tea roses which are still with me; the former's florid blooms distress me, but delight visitors! It has been growing so long that digging it out would disrupt the whole bed; and perhaps it deserves a place for its unswerving flowering loyalty? 'White Swan' is agreeable, though the flowers are shabby after rain, and the moment buds are about to open there is inevitably a downpour. The everlasting pea, *Lathyrus latifolius* 'White Pearl' now grows over it, and the gleaming white pea flowers are good to look at when the roses fade. The 'Superstars' I kindly donated to a less fussy gardener! For a short period I had a white moss rose, so prone to every disease that I think I never saw a properly opened bud.

Rosa glauca has delectable foliage – pinky-green and delicate; the stems are smooth mauve and have a lovely bloom, the growth is very flowing. Flowers and hips are pleasing, but I am prepared to forego these to get lovely fresh, tall stems and this is best achieved by cutting the bush back severely to encourage new growth.

Rosa glauca

Fuchsia
magellanica
'Alba'

Campanula
alliarifolia

Campanula
takesimana

Campanula
trachelium

August

I have not found it an easy subject and have lost several, mainly I think because they have been badly situated, but the present one flourishes in a large pot in the bed in sunlight; much of the base of the pot is cut away to allow for root growth into the garden soil. It shares the pot with a huge self-sown *Helleborus foetidus*, another plant I have found difficult, but these two have become great pot mates. The rose is a martyr to red spider, which mistake my garden for a greenhouse, but I think this is not a common hazard.

Several campanulas (bellflowers) are flowering now – beloved by bees, the heads shrivel as soon as pollinated. By nipping off the faded heads immediately a second crop of flowers can usually be relied upon, extending the pleasure of the flowering season.

The pergola

'Pergola' is a grand name for a double wooden arch which supports a vine – name unknown – that produces a few bunches of grapes each year to delight the birds, and a *Clematis montana*; both of these are very rampant and have to be vigorously restrained as they set off on their headlong course across the flowerbed during the late summer.

They form a frame for the smiling terracotta sun which hangs on the rather dull brick wall that contains the garden on the south-east side. Fortunately in summer the jasmine covers most of the wall; entangled with the gate, it obligingly swings to and fro wafting its sweet scent as the gate is opened or closed.

Climbers on the house wall include *Solanum jasminoides* 'Album', a dainty member of the potato family with a long flowering season, and the unusual dicentra, *D.macrocapnos*, hung with trusses of pale yellow purse-shaped flowers. A clematis from Tashkent is climbing here, grown from a collected seed; hopefully it will flower next year. Clematis grow easily from seed so it is always worth collecting a seedhead, giving the seeds a short spell in an icebox before sowing; germination is quite rapid, and the resulting plant may turn out to be unusual. A shrub which used to be known as *Senecio greyi*, and is now *Brachyglottis* 'Sunshine', is grown here as a climber and in this way displays the white underside of its leaves – as a visitor aptly said 'looking like lots of white kid gloves'. On this same wall in winter the honeysuckle, *Lonicera frag-rantissima*, blooms freely, a large shrub confined to a large pot and firmly pruned to keep it within bounds.

In August in the row of large pots next to the pergola is a tall *Nicotiana sylvestris* and two other tobacco flowers, *N.langsdorffii* and *N.rustica*. An unknown fern spreads its fronds among hellebores. It came unbidden from a nursery in a pot with a camellia – the camellia is long since dead but the fern goes from strength to strength and is much appreciated. Vincas, and in summer nasturtiums, trail over the edges of pots.

Hollyhocks, black and white, grow in the bed where tall plants of *Impatiens glandulifera* flower for a long season, the pale pink flowers continuing their display during July and August and often into September. The tall hybrid tea roses in the bed, 'Gail Borden' and 'White Swan', usually at this time give a second flush. Further back, the plume poppy, *Macleaya cordata*, appreciated for the elegantly shaped leaves, would flourish better given a position in more light, for by late summer its situation is very overshadowed. With space at a premium, it is not always possible to give every plant the situation or the amount of space it deserves.

Clematis montana

Alcea rosea 'Nigra'

Cestrum parqui

Nicotiana sylvestris

Achillea 'Moonshine'

Hosta 'Halcyon'

Colletia paradoxa

Hedera helix 'Ivalace'

Cotoneaster horizontalis

Hydrangea

Tropaeolum

Brachyglottis 'Sunshine'   Dicentra macrocapnos

Nicotiana
viridis.

Solanum jasminoides
'Album'

Nicotiana langsdorffii

Petunia
'Brass Band'

SOLANACEAE

Nicotiana sylvestris

N. glauca

Clematis × jouineana
'Praecox'

Lobelia
'Queen
Victoria'

Eucomis
comosa

August

The window frame in August

Having no space for even the smallest greenhouse is frustrating – however small a garden, there will always be plants requiring protection or attention which it is difficult to provide in their outside situation. Cuttings, seedlings and young plants need warmth and a good light to encourage healthy growth. The contents of a tray of cheerful seedlings left in the open garden will disappear overnight if found by a slug, and a young plant can soon be rendered leafless by a voracious caterpillar.

Years ago I installed a cold frame, but this took up valuable ground space, was not good-looking, and involved a lot of awkward bending as well as providing a breeding place for many pests. Eventually the idea of a glazed frame fitted over my bedroom window, with three adjustable shelves, seemed a good solution. Situated in a good south-west light, with a shelf depth of 15ins (38cm), it accommodates a reasonable number of pots and seed trays. The casement opening can be adjusted to admit air according to the outside temperature, and when tightly closed in winter the frame is just about frostproof. A little extra heat can be added by slightly opening the inside windows, allowing warmth from the flat to leak into the frame. In summer it is mainly used for propagation and in winter it houses tender subjects. At all times the view from the bedroom through the window frame to the garden is very pleasant and the room is filled with a dappled light. An added bonus is that in bad weather the state of the plants can be observed from the inside.

Several times in the year the frame needs a thorough clean: swept first with a small dustpan and soft brush followed by a small battery-operated vacuum cleaner, all residue of soil and dead leaves can easily be removed. About twice a year, after replacing the pots, the use of a smoke fumigant will ensure that all pests on plants or in cracks and crannies will meet their end. Red spider and whitefly are hazards of the window frame, due to the closeness of the plants and the enclosed atmosphere. Recent advice on whitefly suggests that you enlist a helper to disturb the foliage while you aim a vacuum-cleaner nozzle at the airborne insects, instantly sucking them into eternity. The almost invisible red spider is more tenacious; as it dislikes mois-ture a mist spray may help, in addition to specific insecticides, and it is also possible to obtain a control predator to let loose among the enemy. In any contained situation hygiene is essential to counteract mildew and moss and to prevent disease from spreading.

The window frame, without impinging on my space, has solved a number of problems and extended the range of horticultural activities. As it has something of the character of a cottage window, it fits unobtrusively into the garden picture.

Summer bulbs and tubers

In high summer, when growth gets leggy and many of the earlier flowers are already going to seed, summer bulbs help to fill fading areas with strong sculptural shapes and handsome leaves. Started into growth in spring, they are now ready to take their allotted place in the summer scene. *Zantedeschia aethiopica* (arum lilies) are already over but relations such as the delightful *Z.albomaculata* 'Black-eyed Beauty' with spotted leaves are in character at present. The waxy bell-shaped flower of galtonia (summer hyacinth) will grow to 4ft (1.25m); this one is the white *G.candi-*

August

cans, the green-flowered *G.princeps* is a little shorter. Agapanthus is another summer beauty, with which so far I have had little success. *Hymenocallis × festalis* (Spider lily) grown in the window frame until the last minute, is really exotic and its beautiful, complicated flower deserves close inspection.

Tubers of *Begonia × tuberhybrida* are strong growers and the contrasting shapes of the male and female flowers, as well as the leaves, will give fresh life to pots and tubs and once the flowering season has started there is a long succession of blooms. The eucomis family, so seldom seen yet both interesting and rewarding, cannot be overpraised. From the small white *E.zambesiaca* and *E.autumnalis* through to the enormously tall *E.pole-evansii*, all are spectacular and architectural, give height and interest, and look excellent for a long period both in flower and as seedheads. The impressive leaves are often crinkly at the edges, blotched with maroon as in *E.bicolor* or flushed with purple as in the particularly handsome *E.comosa*. Coming from South Africa, eucomis are not hardy, but after allowing the leaves to die down in late autumn the bulbs should be stored dry, away from frost, until next year. As they increase well, a goodly collection will build up year by year.

Galtonia candicans

Eucomis bicolour

Zantedeschia 'Black-eyed Beauty'

Hymenocallis × festalis

Eucomis

Summer bulbs

September

Although leaves on some of the hostas are yellowing, I noticed today that there are flower spikes coming on two of the late flowering varieties, *H.plantaginea* and *H.plantaginea grandiflora* with white and I believe sweet-smelling flowers, which I have yet to see as I was abroad when one of them flowered last year. The former is a division of a root given to me by an old lady, which she brought back from China forty years ago via the Trans-Siberian railway, so it is greatly treasured for its history. *H.plantaginea grandiflora* is from Japan.

The *Skimmia* ssp.*reevesiana* in the side garden has two lots of berries on it at present, still holding last year's red ones but also with a crop of green

Skimmia ssp
reevesiana

ones produced this year. This is a good variety to grow, small, successful in shade and self-fertile, so it is not necessary to provide space for a husband and wife!

Yesterday I clipped the ivy, *Hedera helix* 'Ivalace'; it responds well to this treatment and the resulting neat hard shape contrasts well with the less formal growth around and tightens the corner where it grows under one of the urns. This tightening of some shapes and areas prevents the garden becoming an amorphous mass of foliage.

Peering among plants at the front of the bed I found flower spikes forming on *Saxifraga fortunei* 'Wada'. This dark-leaved saxifrage has myriads of tiny white flowers reminiscent of a flight of

very oversized whitefly! Despite this association it is extremely pretty and delightful to have so late in the year. Looking for the saxifrage reminds me that I should have a labelling session, particularly marking herbaceous plants that disappear completely during winter; it is so easy to forget their positions and to disturb or put a spade through some dormant plant. The disappearance of labels is something of a mystery – for the first Open Day of the year most plants are carefully named, yet a few months later many of the labels have vanished. Now, with the thinning of foliage, it is a good time to sort things out. Many of the marking pens and pencils are so poor that selecting a good one is not always easy – it must be really permanent and the point fine enough to get the complete plant

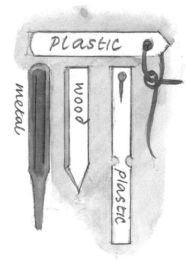

plastic

metal

wood

plastic

75

September

name on the label. Labels with a hole at one end are more useful as they can be tied with garden string to bushes and twiners or to the trellis where they are growing; they can also be inserted into pots, but something more substantial is needed to push into the soil of the flowerbed, and either wooden or metal labels are more satisfactory. Names can be checked for spelling and accuracy in *The Plant Finder* (see below and page 108). Small pots sometimes get overlooked; this can be disastrous, as what is mistaken for an empty pot of soil and tipped away may contain seeds or bulbs which may be lost for good. The plant list I keep is useful to fall back on as a reminder of forgotten names – it was started when I first opened the garden as a check when visitors asked for information, and I have since realized how useful it is.

Plant names have a disconcerting habit of changing and here again *The Plant Finder* is useful. This annual publication is a directory that accurately lists about sixty thousand plants and gives information about the nurseries where they may be obtained, either by a visit or by mail order. If the grower is an exhibitor at

R.H.S. shows, plants ordered may usually be collected there. Another source for collectors of the unusual is at garden Open Days when some owners devote a small corner or table to selling rooted cuttings from their own gardens at a modest price, usually for charity.

Light in the garden

Just as light in the theatre can illuminate a scene in many different ways, so in the garden one should take notice of how the light falls at different times of day and at different times of the year, and also of the quality of light, whether it is the full bright light of midday, the dappled light of moving trees and the leaves of creepers, the soft light of dawn or the grey light of evening. Light shining through leaves and petals may give

quite a different colour to the plant or, silhouetted against the sun, the pattern of the leaves and twigs will emphasize their skeletal design. Against a dark and stormy sky, colours can appear dramatically and weirdly different.

At present, in the late afternoon the light slants across the garden and gives the golden privet a glowing golden light, emphasizing the grace of its growth. So often this well-known bush is grown as a hedge and clipped severely back, which makes it look very uninteresting. Carefully pruned, it sprays out its well-shaped oval leaves with distinction.

The privet contrasts well with the angular growth of the *Pyracantha* 'Golden Charmer' covered with not-too-garish orange berries until the birds enjoy the feast. The *Nicotiana glauca* (see page 71) is now about 5ft (1.5m) tall and the trumpet flowers are a warm yellow, unlike the lime yellow of its relations. From the workroom window, this grouping presents a pattern of shapes and colour that is very satisfying. The hosta in the tub below the privet is 'Zounds', one of the few that hold their yellow colour throughout the season.

Pyracantha
'golden
Charmer'

Nicotiana
glauca

Fuchsia
'Whirlaway'

Mahonia
japonica

Hosta erromena

Colletia
paradoxa

Hosta
sieboldiana

Epimedium
pewalderianum

Choisya ternata
'Sundance'

Leaves in a cool corner – smooth and prickly.
In the urn, *Hosta erromena*; in deep shade,
H.sieboldiana; the three-fingered leaves of
Choisya ternata stretch out towards the sun

September

Smooth and prickly

As the summer progresses, the area around the mahonia becomes very shady so that the urn cannot be planted with bedding subjects or anything needing good light. For several years now two hostas, *H.erromena* and *H.*'Variegata', have shared the space, and have flourished so well that this year it will be necessary to divide the roots before they become pot-bound. In the deep shade, fewer flower spikes are produced than on many of the hostas in lighter positions. In the spring, before the hosta leaves appear, three pale yellow hyacinths light up this corner and are removed immediately after flowering. In midsummer, as a contrast to the sturdy shape of the hostas, either a white-flowered *Begonia semperflorens* or a white-flowered *Impatiens sultanii* is introduced to the pot and usually performs well for a few months, seeming not to mind the gloom. The pot is overhung by the mahonia, which spreads its pinnate spiney leaves about it in graceful layers. In the bed below the mahonia is *Hosta sieboldiana*, with large, impressive grey-blue glaucus leaves and pure white flowers – greatly preferable to the more usual washed-out mauvey-grey flowers of most of the family. This plant has increased so substantially that pieces of it have been given to many friends. The spiky leaves of the mahonia are shed freely on everything below and need to be removed from the hosta leaves before inflicting damage.

Along the low brick wall surrounding the flowerbed are several epimediums – three heart-shaped leaves spring from each dark wiry stem – and if the old leaves are cut away in spring the sprays of tiny flowers are better displayed. Some forms of epimedium have leaves that take on bronze colouring during the winter months.

Nearby, the most dangerously prickly plant I know is the South American *Colletia paradoxa* – the triangular spines of dark leaden green are very decorative. In November flowers similar to lily-of-the-valley are borne, which smell very sweetly.

In front of this, where it catches some sunshine, is the golden-leaved *Choisya ternata* 'Sundance' – not reliably hardy, so in need of a sheltered spot or some winter protection. Apart from the hostas, all these subjects are evergreen, giving a permanent pattern of interesting shapes.

Fuchsias and begonias

The great advantage of both fuchsias and begonias is that they come into flower at the end of the summer when the garden begins to look tired, and will continue manfully until the frosts – providing that, in the case of fuchsias, the seed pods are removed.

In damp grey weather fuchsias are still successful, for they prefer a damp atmosphere and need plenty of moisture, soon drooping the moment their compost becomes dry. The variety of fuchsias available is daunting; immense displays are set up by growers of more and more cultivars, many of them reminiscent of fat ballet dancers or ladies overdressed for a garden party. Of the hardy fuchsias, I have two growing here in the bed: *F.magellanica* 'Alba', which will grow into a large bush of very pale pink small flowers that make a long and continuous display; and *F.*'Hawkshead', whose similarly shaped flowers, white with green tips, are even more subtle and which begins to bloom later in the season but continues for a long time. If cut back by frost in winter new growth will emerge in spring, and for my purposes, to keep the bushes small, I always prune them back severely early in the year.

Fuchsia 'Thalia'.

Begonia sutherlandii

Begonia x
tuberhybrida

F. 'White
Spider'

F. magellanica 'Alba'

F. 'Hawkshead'

Fuchsia
'Billy
Green'

Begonia semperflorens

September

The other fuchsias are wintered in the window frame, kept very dry, and go into wall-hangers as they come into bloom. The simpler varieties suit my garden; those with florid flowers, full of petals, seem to me to lack the natural elegance of the genus.

Fuchsias strike easily from cuttings, or will even root in a jar of water. Another hint received from a fuchsia nurseryman is to plant deep; this encourages the side shoots to root and they can then be severed from the plant.

Both tuberous- and fibrous-rooted begonias have a long flowering span and are easy to grow, and many have very handsome leaves. The tubers, if stored in a dry and airy situation, can be used year after year and so are very economical. Although the fibrous-rooted *B.semperflorens* can last through the winter in ideal conditions – maybe on a light window sill – buying new ones each year is inexpensive and young plants are more shapely.

The little pendulous *Begonia sutherlandii* is a charmer; the tuber lasts from year to year, and in the leaf axils new little tubers are formed which, if carefully picked off at the end of the autumn and sprinkled onto a pot of compost, will sprout in late spring, and the new crop of plants will flower by late summer.

September flowers

Much as I particularly love the Japanese anemone, *Anemone hupehensis*, the appearance of its flowers in the garden is the first intimation of autumn, with the suggestion of yellowing and falling leaves and the approach of chilly days. These anemones range from white to deep pink and may be single or double, but the purity and stateliness of the single white form is unsurpassed. They increase readily from a creeping root stock, but are slow to establish and after planting rarely produce flowers until the second year. From then on they can be relied upon for a steady performance.

A climber that will grow from seed to a good height in its first year is *Cobaea scandens* (cup-and-saucer plant, or cathedral bells), which starts flowering in early autumn and will continue to produce its strange greeny-purple flowers until the frost cuts it down. The colour variation as the flowers change from green to purple is beautiful to watch, and there is a pale greeny-white form as well. Seed pods are often produced and the seeds germinate much more frequently than those from a packet. Sow in gentle heat in March, planting the seeds on edge after they have been soaked for a few hours. The plant climbs by tendrils from the ends of the leaves.

One of the prettiest clematis is *C.'Alba Luxurians'* in flower from July to September; the charmingly-shaped single white flowers are tipped with green and are very variable in shape – a plant for the connoisseur, a retiring beauty.

Clematis 'Alba Luxurians'

Cobaea scandens

Anemone hupehensis

October

DIARY
3 October – planting bulbs and using discrimination

The stores are full of bulbs to be planted now for spring flowering. They should be chosen with care from the considerable hotch-potch on view. My white and lemon hyacinths should be in the earth this week, which means a clearing of the urns and bowls for which they are destined, exchanging some of the spent compost worn out by summer flowerers with some fresh material to give the bulbs a good start. Plants that live permanently in the containers, such as hostas, *Dicentra formosa* and *Alyssum saxatile*, can be carefully lifted out and separated where necessary before replacing. The old compost, together with falling leaves, will be dumped in the compost bin. This is too small to take all the autumn refuse and the excess must go into sacks to be sent to the tip. A great help in clearing up is the use of a strong plastic garden 'hold-all' either spread under the area which is being cut back or, if a smaller version, located close enough to the work area for all the debris to be thrown in – thus saving back-breaking sweeping and gathering up of piles of clippings.

As the evergreen foliage comes into its own, it becomes clear how valuable some variegated foliage can be at this time of year. *Elaeagnus pungens* 'Maculata' gleams with sharp brilliance, looking always as though it is caught in a beam of sunlight. Variegated hollies add texture as well as colour, particularly the hedgehog-like leaves of *Ilex aquifolium* 'Ferox Argentea'. Some variegated ivies lighten dark corners.

garden 'hold-all'

Variegation in excess can be busy and formless and should be used with discrimination as it can destroy both form and shape – there are multi-coloured roses in which form and petal shape are totally lost. Discrimination is a quality lacking among gardeners who see their domain as a horn of plenty, rioting with herbage and colour. It is also important to be discriminating in the choice of plants – some gardeners must have one of everything and especially of rarities unknown to their neighbours, regardless of the performance and aesthetic qualities of the subject, resulting in a gabble of plants like a crowd of ill-assorted people trying to draw attention to themselves. 'A garden is a lovesome thing' – but not if it is a battleground for the less-than-choice.

DIARY
14 October – collecting seeds

Now is the time to keep an eye on ripening seeds which have been earmarked for collection with a view to sowing next year. Saving seeds from plants for personal propagation is great fun and the idea of perpetuating an old friend fits in well with the idea of a garden being a place of regeneration and tradition.

It is important that the seeds are ripe – which means that they should be on the point of bursting out of the seedcase themselves without help. This entails constant observation or the seeds may have taken propagation into their own hands. Daily inspection is advised! At the right moment, the seedhead may be snipped off the stalk with sharp scissors straight into a paper envelope; the seeds can be shaken loose and the debris of the seed container then disposed of. Some plants such as papaver (poppy)

October

tropaeolum

papaver

collecting seed

and nicotiana (tobacco) will provide thousands of seeds and they self-seed prolifically. *N.glauca* is the only one at the moment that I am saving for myself and friends. As the nasturtiums here are all pale yellow, these seeds are collected: they cannot be guaranteed to come true but enough for my needs are likely to be of the same strain, and interlopers can be weeded out to prevent cross-fertilization. These large seeds have a tendency to topple off and must often be gathered from the ground beneath the trailing leaves. As they are still green they should be left to dry off on a small tray and only stored when quite dry.

Some bulbs such as galtonia and eucomis have fine seedpods. The three or four years required to grow these to flowering size is not very practical unless there is plenty of room for developing plants.

Seeds of admired plants given by friends are always welcome and forge a link between gardens, and seeds brought back from far-off lands add excitement. Argemone seeds brought back from Sa'ana in the Yemen have produced some of the prettiest leaves imaginable, and a plantago grown from seeds brought from Kunming in China is looking healthy – not a plant one would cross the world to get, but a happy reminder of an interesting journey.

Seed-saving and gathering is the most economical way of increasing plants when purchased packets of seed can make quite a hole in the pocket – and, what is more, there is no doubt that the seed is fresh!

Argemone
(from Sa'aana)

October garden – the long view

Visitors enter the main part of the garden through the gate that separates it from the side garden, and their first sight of the main garden is the 'long view'. (I tend not to think of the side garden as part of the main garden, because, although it contains some quite interesting plants, it is mainly a passageway.)

Friends come into the garden through the workroom french windows and are met by an entirely different aspect, short and wide. Strangely, the 'long view' seen from the gate is rarely lingered over – visitors seem impelled to move on, taking a stance in the middle – yet it is interesting as a vista and worth pausing over. For one thing, it has no end, for the fence is completely curtained in climbers and no buildings interrupt the view of distant tall trees and an expanse of sky.

As the eye is allowed to wander, the garden is seen framed in the arch or 'mini pergola', heavily burdened at this time of year with *Clematis montana* frantically throwing out strands of new growth and the not very fruitful vine beginning to yellow overhead. Pots hang on the uprights of the arch, changed according to season and at present holding an interesting polygonum with pewter-green leaves splashed with maroon, turning brilliant red in autumn.

October

The eye passes over the flower-bed to the left, with *Helleborus arguti-folius* and *Cotoneaster horizontalis*, to a bank of plants and small bushes crowned with a lace-cap hydrangea and the prettily yellowing, willow-shaped leaves of *Cestrum parqui*, behind which a pink *Ribes* and the winter jasmine (*Jasminum nudiflorum*) share a chimneypot with splendid abandon. The jardinière stands between this pot bank and one that includes a handsome *Euphorbia mellifera* and the spiky *Poncirus* (hardy orange). To the right glows the 'dark drift', leading onwards over jasmine and clematis to the distant background of tall trees.

October leaves and tones

Coming through the side gate this morning, a conflagration of reds glowed across the garden. Surrounded by so much evergreen foliage, an area that has changed colour dramatically becomes a very arresting accent. The 'dark drift', which gives depth to one of the pot banks throughout the year, is at present glowing with red and purple. Its colours are richer than in previous years: this may be due to re-angling the bank of pots so that it now faces due south. The extent to which plants colour in autumn depends on the amount of light they receive and the air temperature, and this slight change of direction seems to have benefited the plants gathered together here. The brown leaves of *Cordyline australis* and of *Carex petriei* will of course be retained through the winter but the – at present – theatrically coloured leaves of *Darmera peltata* will shortly fall and it will not put up its fresh green umbrellas again until after the pink flower spikes in spring. The round darmera leaves are pleasantly echoed by the circular *Aeonium arboreum* and the softly scalloped leaves of the heuchera 'Pewter Moon'. Tall beetroot-coloured stems of *Lobelia* 'Queen Victoria' carry brilliant red insect-like flowers, which should look wrong in this garden but are surprisingly successful in this context. This is not a plant to stand cold weather so it will be removed after flowering and stowed at the back of one of the shelves underneath the window frame; this way it has so far survived several winter seasons. The leaves of a newly acquired *Euphorbia dulcis* 'Chameleon' are of the richest brown madder; hopefully it will retain its neat compact shape. Below it a similarly coloured *Euonymus nanus* var. *turkestanicus* spreads small branches of narrow leaves, to be held throughout the winter.

Graceful among the background climbers are the trailing stems of filigree silver leaves of *Artemisia arborescens*, which, having survived a mild winter, have spread out over a considerable distance. *Helichrysum petiolare* and *H.p.* 'Limelight' spill over from hanging pots, giving sparkle among fading leaves of clematis and the rambling rose 'Félicité et Perpétue'. Many grey-leaved plants are hardy and hold their leaves throughout the winter, providing a valuable contrast both in colour and texture to the heavier colour of the evergreen foliage, especially satisfactory in the low-level light of a dark winter's day. Interesting balance between light and dark is an important aspect of picture-making in the garden.

Lobelia
'Queen
Victoria'

Hydrangea serrata
'Preziosa'

Carex.
petriei

Cordyline australis

Euphorbia dulcis
'Chamelion'

Darmera peltata

Heuchera 'Pewter Moon'

October

Hosta plantaginea grandiflora

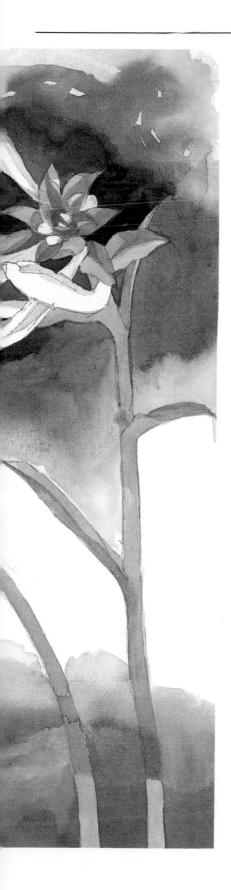

Hosta plantaginea grandiflora

The very handsome and desirable *Hosta plantaginea grandiflora* is stunning in the autumn garden. Fresh green deeply-ridged leaves are surmounted by flower spikes bearing large pure white flowers which radiate from the stem. I am now able to testify that, as I had hoped, these are deliciously and powerfully scented. Flowering is so late in the year – which is in itself a bonus – that they should have a warm and sunny position so that the flowers, which might not develop properly in the shade, will give an excellent display. In bad weather the pot can be brought indoors, where, in a cool place, the flowers will open unspoiled by wind and rain and the room will be suffused with the magic scent.

Seedheads

In a large garden in autumn the emphasis is on textured bark, coloured stems such as the various forms of *Cornus*, and misty vistas coloured in gold, bronze and lemon by leaves and, of course, seedheads. In the small garden, although there is not room to plan for this, some of the shrubs and plants grown will delight briefly with autumn colours, and quite a number of subjects, annual and perennial, will have seedheads to be enjoyed. Looking at the dried-out plants ('dead' seems the wrong word to choose) one can appreciate the strength and design of the skeletal structure.

The hydrangea heads are gradually changing their colour; the mop-heads of *H.serrata* 'Preziosa' spectacularly become a deep maroon, the lace-caps are paper-brown and the spidery heads of *H.petiolaris* are very distinctive. Leaving heads on hydrangeas also affords a little protection to next year's shoots.

All the varieties of acanthus are good in autumn, the spikes surviving well and spitting out large mahogany-coloured seeds to ensure plenty of new plants. The leaves, which are prone to mildew, can be disposed of in the compost bin.

One of the loveliest plants in its winter state is *Molucella laevis* (Bells of Ireland), grown annually not for its insignificant flowers but for the shapely bracts like the horns of early gramophones in miniature. The pincushion heads of *Astrantia*, the masses of pods on the perennial sweet pea, *Lathyrus latifolius*, and the russetting fern fronds are decorative and, briefly, there are hosta leaves turning golden. *Lunaria* (honesty) is a mass of silver moons, and silky catherine wheels are decorating the clematis before the wind whirls them away.

Overleaf **October seedheads**

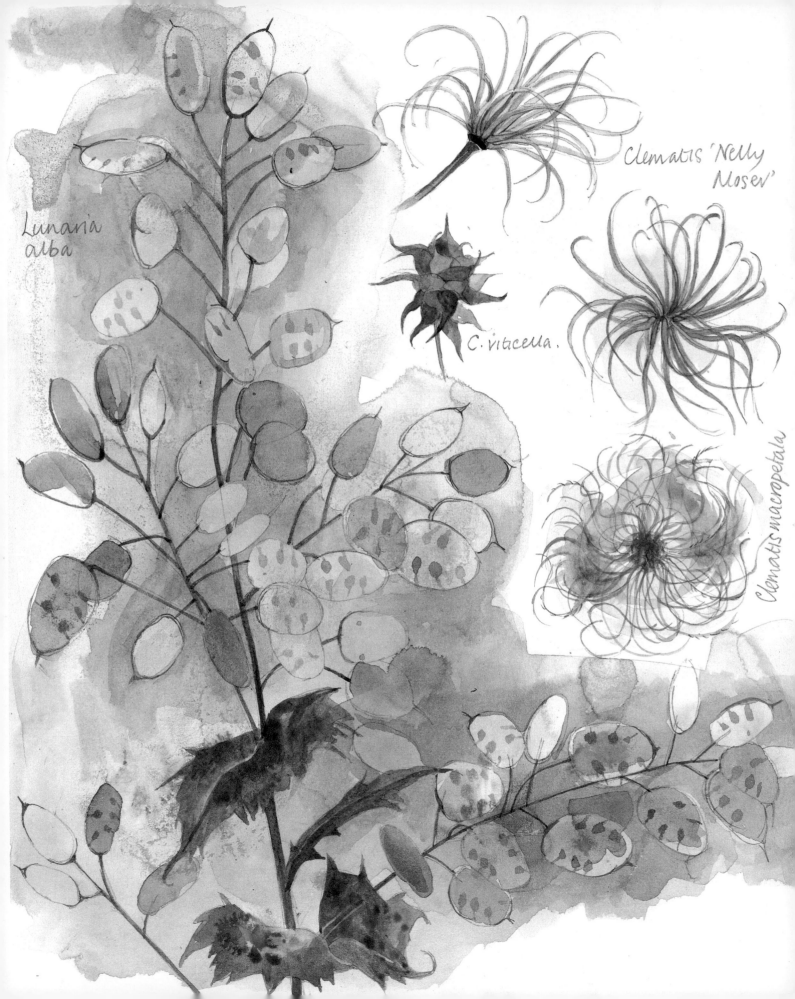

Lunaria
alba

Clematis 'Nelly
Moser'

C. viticella.

Clematis macropetala

Astrantia

Acanthus
mollis.

Iris
foetidissima

Molucella

Hydrangea
Petiolaris

November

Tulipa 'Red Riding Hood'

It is time for the early winter clearance of the window frame, to make as much room as possible for tender plants which will need space there shortly. Although I prefer to leave half-hardy subjects outside, receiving natural rainfall and a better circulation of air, until the last possible moment, it is easy to be caught out by a sudden cold snap and find oneself in the dusk with frozen fingers gathering together pots to save them from an untimely death. If the plants have been trimmed back and tidied in preparation for their move there will be no need for hasty snipping at the last moment.

The species tulips bought last month at the Royal Horticultural Society's Great Autumn Show were planted in pots this morning and can be stood in a corner of the garden where they will get rained on and be cold enough not to start shooting too soon. They can be put under shelter for forcing in a couple of months' time.

It is good to be able to see the bones of the garden again and to appreciate shapes that have recently been masked by the excessive growth of some climbers – for example, *Clematis armandii* and *C. montana* which have sent out strands in all directions. Some plants, too, have been buried by other growth – *Houttuynia cordata* 'Flore Pleno' and *Lamium galeobdolon* 'Florentinum' are running about everywhere and much needs to be removed. I am also in the process of tidying and sorting out growth on the south-east-facing fence – the fence itself disappeared under its burden of greenery years ago – where the ivy *Hedera helix* 'Glacier', with grey-green leaves edged in white, *Jasminum officinale*, *Clematis × jouiniana* 'Praecox' and the rambler rose 'Félicité et Perpétue' all need restraining so that the less-overpowering plants have a fair chance of flourishing.

Sniffing the air there seemed to be a possibility of frost, so I have been busy giving some protection to the more tender plants with onion sacks, which can be picked up when I am passing through the nearby street market. Because of the nature of the mesh, they give protection while allowing a circulation of air. Some pots are just dropped gently into the sacks which are then tied at the tops. Larger subjects can be covered by opening up the seams of the bags, laying them over or around the plants and either tying them around with string or clipping with clothes pegs. In the case of climbers, the protection

onion sack protection

clothes peg.

can be pegged or tied to the supporting trellis. The garden looks rather curious in its wrappings but not as curious, perhaps, as another garden I know whose owner wraps her most precious plants in discarded woollen sweaters!

Because so much of the garden is contained in pots, the real hazard is that the containers may freeze solid. In this condition the roots are unable to take in any moisture and the plants virtually die of drought; in some fleshy-rooted plants the cell structure of the root breaks down and disintegrates into a mushy mess. Clustering pots together and protecting with thick wads of newspaper is a help, and if possible packing them with some straw, dried leaves or bracken. Plastic bubble-wrap can also be wound round the pots, but it is not advisable completely to envelop plants in any kind of plastic as this causes condensation and the confined damp air encourages mildew and rotting.

In the gardens of north China, where the winters are very hard, pots often have rope wound tightly round them to provide the necessary protection. As the plants in many of the pots look very ancient this must be a successful method, although achieving it appears to be a fine art and the result of years of training and expertise. The ropework is left permanently in place, becomes weathered and is very agreeable to look at.

leaf and bracken
protection.

Plants in November
The garden in November varies greatly from year to year, depending on the autumn weather. Here, in central London, frosts do not usually strike severely until after Christmas and in a sheltered garden a number of late summer favourites – even bedding plants such as pelargoniums and petunias – may still be producing desultory blossoms, and some deciduous plants are slow to lose their leaves in a mild autumn.

Abelia grandiflora is still producing a few flowers, white with a touch of pink, and the pinkish brown sepals are a feature of this plant. The small airy bush arches gracefully and is perhaps best appreciated freestanding in a large pot, where it is likely to live happily for twenty years or so. Some years, as at present, the shiny light green leaves become suffused with soft red so that the entire bush blushes delicately. Although classed as deciduous, the two I have growing here, *A. × grandiflora* and *A. × grandiflora* 'Francis Mason', have retained their leaves.

The mop-head hydrangea, *H. serrata* 'Preziosa', is a chameleon plant. The flowerheads when they first open are a brilliant limey green, developing into a pink so shocking as to transfix all who see it, and then gradually it assumes a brown-red of great richness and the leaves turn from dark red to purple. This small bush is essential in a grouping of dark plants. Like all hydrangeas it needs to be well watered and in my experience it is a slow starter.

On either side of the workroom window, pots contain the slightly tender *Correa*, not much seen, possibly

Correa
backhouseana

Correa
alba

Hydrangea
serrata 'Preziosa'

Abelia x grandiflora

November

because of its tenderness, but facing south against a wall mine have flourished splendidly. The oval ever-green leaves are pale underneath and the stems a light ochre colour. There is a long flowering season from October to March with a succession of small bell-shaped flowers – almost white with recurved petals in *C.alba*, and a pale browny-green dusted with tiny brown spots in *C.backhouseana*. These are plants I would not be without and if really bitter cold strikes it is always feasible to cover them with a protective mesh stretched across and clipped to the support with clothes pegs for the duration of the bad weather. In the years that these have grown in the garden the largest has once been repotted, but there has never been any need to prune or even tidy the bushes – their growth is impeccable.

Berries and birds

The traditional colour of autumn is briefly reflected here in the several kinds of coloured berries, which will last until the birds have gorged them-selves. They tie in nicely with the yellowing leaves which will drop so quickly and damply if it rains, or be whirled away by gusts of wind. Each year at leaf-fall I hope that the wind will be from the south-east so that the thousands of leaves from nearby trees will not be deposited, knee deep, into the garden.

The *Cotoneaster horizontalis* immediately outside the workroom window is a mass of berries, and shortly the leaves will turn bright scarlet too, dropping to reveal the fishbone skeleton of the bush, which can continue to hold its berries after the leaves have gone providing the marauding birds do not arrive too early! This plant was grown from a

cutting which was covered with large stones to provide a cool root run, and the resulting bush never fails to per-form; only the increase in size pre-sents problems. At flowering time it is a mass of bees.

The potted *Pyracantha* 'Golden Charmer' has, unlike its much older sister in the side garden, produced masses of berries from the start, and its corner position in front of one of the tall chimneypots was a good choice. Alas, it too is very attractive to birds and, although regrettable, their busy antics as they go to work strip-ping it of berries are very entertaining to watch. The visiting birds are only of common varieties but their activity throughout the winter adds another dimension to the garden's interest, and the different heights of the plants and their containers provide them with perches at every level. The arrival

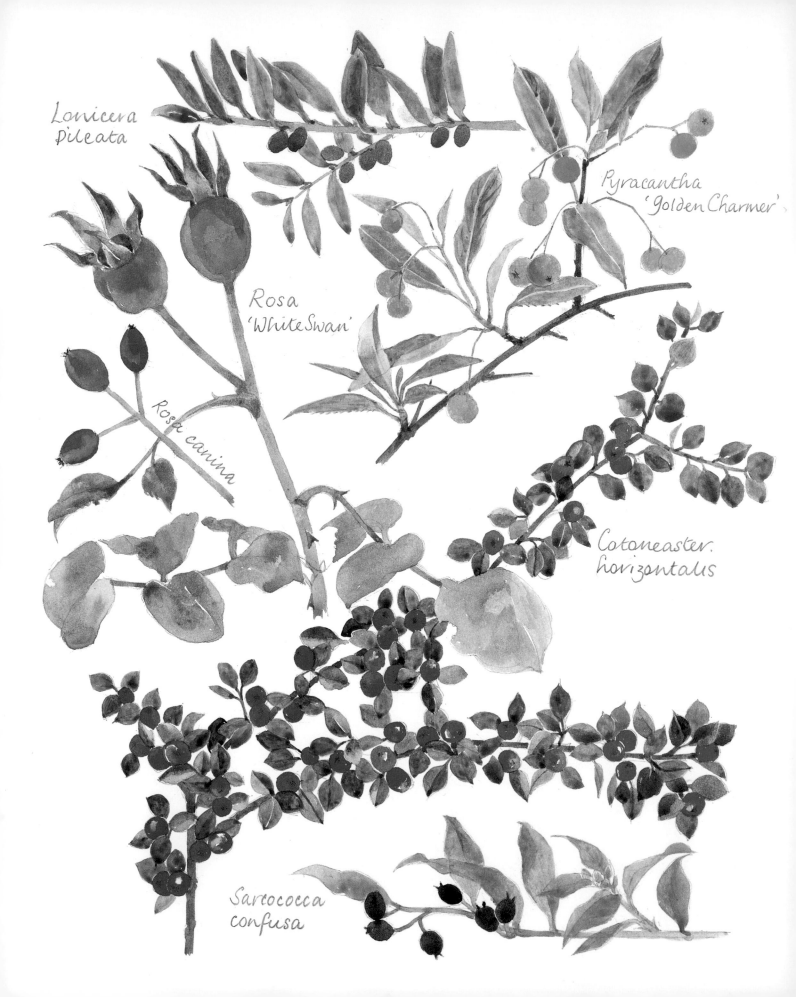

Lonicera
pileata

Pyracantha
'golden Charmer'

Rosa
'White Swan'

Rosa canina

Cotoneaster.
horizontalis

Sarcococca
confusa

November

of an occasional wood pigeon in so small a space is rather like a jumbo jet dropping in!

All the sarcococcas I grow have black berries. Those on *S.confusa* turn dark red at first; they are usually still on the bushes as the flower buds form, and the bushes frequently have flowers and berries together.

Glassy, translucent purple berries are produced by *Lonicera pileata*, a spring-flowering honeysuckle that is prostrate in form and here spreads small shiny leaves over the edge of a large pot. It is not fussy about growing conditions, and although not profligate with its berries it is a plant worth having.

Rose hips can be very spectacular and the shapes and colours vary greatly. This year *Rosa glauca* is devoid of fruit, but 'White Swan' has a crop of chubby hips. Those on the wild rose, *R.canina*, tend to prefer the railway line to the garden and are, I hope, delighting the passengers as they approach their destination.

Mahonia

The *Mahonia japonica* (Bealei Group) grows at the back of the flowerbed to a height of about 10ft (3m), spreading its grey-green prickly leaves rhythmically like the waves of the sea. From the ends of its branches – officially in late autumn but sometimes earlier – pale yellow sprays of small flowers fill the air with a scent like lilies-of-the-valley that pervades the garden deliciously. Both the flowers and the scent can be enjoyed through several winter months. In early summer, as the flowers fade, small bunches of grape-like berries covered with a dark blue bloom develop, and for a while are very decorative. Then I am aware of a rustling and shaking of leaves and I know that the blackbird is in the depth of the bush systematically stripping it of berries; there is an occasional flurry as a rival tries to join

Mahonia
haematocarpa

the feast and is quickly seen off, and the shining blackbird with its gleaming eye gets to work again. Mahonia prunings are reputed to root very easily; it is surprising to find when making any cuts that the inner wood is bright yellow! Old leaves sometimes colour beautifully, but individually, not *en masse*, and the lower stems eventually become bare, but this is a bush which sprouts well from the base. The shed leaves are a prickly hazard at leaf clearing time.

Among the many forms of mahonia, I grow one – *Mahonia haematocarpa* – that is little seen elsewhere; as it is grown in a pot it remains quite small, and it is surprising to find it can grow into a sizeable shrub. The prickly leaves are small and grey-green, almost glaucous. Yellow flowers arrive in summer, followed by juicy orange-red berries. It needs a sheltered and warm position as it is not totally hardy and may need cossetting in bad weather, but it is worth the trouble for it is a very pretty bush.

Mahonia japonica
Bealei Group

December

The dying back of herbaceous subjects opens up the garden for a few months – particularly the flowerbed – and reveals the earth which has been covered over for so many months. At this time ground cover is much appreciated – and probably the ground cover itself is appreciating the light and air and rain that is now reaching it! The driest part of the bed, under the mahonia, comes into view and it is cheering that *Luzula* 'Variegata' (guaranteed to flourish in these conditions) is establishing well and that some rooted pieces of *Euphorbia robbiae*, transplanted from a better-placed clump, have settled down. *Brunnera macrophylla* from a friend's garden is spreading, though the leaf markings are less evident than in the parent. The tiny bronze-leaved *Acaena* gets very smothered in the bed in summer but the pieces planted in a large pot beneath *Brachyglottis* 'Sunshine' are making growth.

All the epimediums make excellent winter cover, and little clumps of the grass *Milium effusum* 'Aureum' survive brightly. Stiff blades of *Acorus calamus* 'Variegatus' fan out from their pot and other pot-grown grasses, *Festuca glauca* and *Carex petriei*, make useful sharp shapes. Several evergreen ferns are making slow growth.

Saxifraga umbrosa (London Pride) and another saxifrage, *S. × andrewsii* with a leaf edge that might have been cut with dressmaker's pinking shears, are tough enough to survive any conditions; *S.cuscutiformis*, which in summer has delicate sprays of tiny white moth-like flowers, will come through the cold months too and has sent out runners with a plantlet dangling on the end of each.

Saxifraga cuscutiformis.

All the year round there are opportunities to observe, read and think about gardens and to exercise that seeing eye when looking at pictures in galleries and books, but more especially so in winter when there is less opportunity to work outside. The shelves in libraries and bookshops are crowded with works that will instruct, enthuse and elucidate. Many of these, despite the attractive photographs and descriptions of important and well-set-out gardens, are very alike in content; many will advise on which colours to put together, on ideal tub and window-box plantings, in fact exactly how the garden should look, disregarding the personal touch that is the essence of individual success.

Every gardener needs a bookshelf, though it need not be so very crowded, but each book, like the plants, should be well chosen and loved and a friend. These good companions for everyday will help one choose plants wisely and understand the conditions they need, to know how large they will grow and when to expect them to flower. A comprehensive and reliable encyclopedia makes working in the garden and looking at plants much more interesting, and the works of some good writers such as Vita Sackville-West, Christopher Lloyd and Graham Stuart Thomas will much enrich understanding. For the bedside table, books by and about plant hunters will recount where and how plants were discovered and make fascinating reading.

But I am also thinking of books and pictures across a wider spectrum. Pictures of gardens can be found everywhere to provoke thought and inspiration, throwing quite a different slant on design from that received when looking at other people's gardens, however excellent they may be. For example, Mughal miniature paintings are rich in garden information exquisitely depicted. There are frescoes in the tombs and temples of Egypt showing charming gardens where amphorae and flowerpots edge walks and form patterns surrounded by plantings of formal trees. Chinese and Japanese screens are painted, if not with entire gardens, with groupings and arrangements of plants emphasizing flower and leaf shapes,

Egyptian fresco - vases lining steps.

Medieval wattle fence

sometimes in conjunction with rocks or stones or twisted branches. French tapestries have backdrops spangled with tiny flowers, and in medieval manuscripts ladies sit in gardens full of flowers enclosed by walls and plaited wattle fences where decorative small trees and climbers are trained into formal shapes. Roman mosaic pavements can inspire with designs, as in a smaller and more informal way

can the pebble patterns in Chinese gardens, and there is additional food for thought in renaissance plans of parterres, mazes and knot gardens.

All these are riches to be pondered over, digested and selected – it is not, for instance, necessary to recreate a Persian garden, but fragments of colour, shape and texture from miniatures should invade the gardener's thinking.

Nor is the past the only source of inspiration, for the drawings (and writings) of Paul Klee, and of many other abstract painters, will furnish ideas for colour, shape and pattern that can be integrated into even the smallest back yard.

Pebble roundel

Fisherman's garden. Suzou.

Elaeagnus
pungens
'Maculata'

Lamium
galeobdolon
'Florentinum'

Sinarundinaria nitida

December

December backdrop

Besides the climbers and scramblers used for clothing the garden's perimeters, some free-standing shrubs are worth considering. On a dull overcast day *Elaeagnus pungens* 'Maculata', noted in October, is still fresh and bright. This stiff, crisp bush has ovate leathery leaves with a splash of yellow in the centre and a crinkly edging of olive green. Whatever the weather, the eleagnus can be relied upon to withstand it – I think there is no other bush in the garden so reliable in performance. The undersides of the leaves are a matt buff colour in contrast to the shiny brilliance of the upper side. For a garden this size it needs constant cutting back and does not resent it; also, as some shoots revert to plain green, these too must be removed. In the fifteen years I have possessed it, it has only berried once – a big crop, dull red, pendulous and insignificant.

Also forming part of the backdrop is one of the smaller and less invasive bamboos, *Sinarundinaria nitida*, which forms a charming and impenetrable thicket. Frequently depicted in Chinese paintings, the leaves of these oriental plants are sharply pointed and angular like brush strokes and the slender, tapering stems, growing very close together, are made decorative by their nubbly joints. This spreading plant will grow to about 10ft (3m) and, though not nearly as rampant as most bamboos, will need occasional root pruning, when it may be necessary to use an axe to sever the culms. The plant is so handsome that it is worth the effort! Like the eleagnus, the bamboo is good looking in winter and weatherproof. The old stems, though not as tough as shop-bought canes, make excellent supports for smaller plants.

In front of these is the green rose *R.*'Viridiflora', little seen or known but with some charm and a habit of carrying flowers throughout the year; these are not at all showy and the rather ragged petals have a touch of maroon, giving them a bronzy look.

Running about the ground is *Lamium galeobdolon* 'Florentinum', which is INVASIVE! It provides decorative ground cover in winter when much of the earth is bare, the well-shaped green leaves have central splashes of silver-grey that are well defined. In early summer there are yellow nettle-like flowers, and the plant is worth growing provided that some of the long runners that root wherever they touch the ground are constantly reduced.

Rosa 'White Swan' - December 25th

Ilex aquifolium
'Argentea marginata'

Hedera helix
'Glacier'

Hedera helix
'Goldheart'

Citrus paradisi

Ilex
meserveae
'Blue Angel'

December

Christmas tree: the garden comes indoors

Brought indoors for Christmas, the grapefruit tree sparkles, decorated with red and pink and sometimes silver glass balls. Grown from a pip and now 5ft (1.5m) high, it stands on a table in front of the window and the dark, leathery green leaves give off a smell of citrus in the warm air of the room. The tree must stand away from any direct or drying heat which would shrivel the leaves, and because it is contained in a small pot it must be frequently watered. Scale insects are a particular pest of citrus trees and this is a good opportunity to remove them either by rubbing them off with the fingers, or touching them with a brush dipped in methylated spirits.

Before the grapefruit grew large enough to support its Christmas burden, a bay tree held pride of place; its rather similar dark green leaves, spicily scented, showed off the baubles equally well and, like the grapefruit tree, it was always admired. These trees seem to me much superior to the commonly used spruce, which sheds its needles and ends up sadly dead, and they can be returned to the garden in all their plain undecorated green ness when the festive season is over.

The very small garden will not provide an abundance of seasonal greenery, but here, where ivy abounds on the surrounding walls and fences, it is possible to cut a bunch without denuding the view. In most profusion is the Irishman's ivy, *Hedera* 'Hibernica', which can beneficially be cut back; and a very spreading *H.helix* 'Glacier' sends out such long strands that a winter pruning is not detrimental. Used in an arrangement, the bright leaves of *H.helix* 'Goldheart' splashed with buttercup yellow look well with a few sprigs of *Elaeagnus pungens* 'Maculata'. Two other dark green ivies – the crimpy 'Ivalace' and the thin-fingered 'Sagittifolia' add other leaf shapes. The three hollies that are planted in the half barrel are so slow-growing that they will have to be left alone for many years, but *Ilex × meserveae* 'Blue Angel' has put on more growth and, as it is in a small pot, it can come inside and stand on a table; the glossy, dark leaves are almost navy blue and are a fine foil for its crop of red berries, which the birds either have not found or do not like. Sometimes at Christmas I have been able to gather the green rose 'Viridiflora' and the hybrid tea 'White Swan' which is often blooming in late December. With a sprig or two of winter jasmine and a few snippets of sweet-smelling mahonia a small bunch can be put together for a place on the dining table.

Plant list

This is a list of some favourite and less commonly grown plants that flourish in this small urban garden, most of which are mentioned in the text.

Climbers
Akebia quinata
Clematis armandii
Clematis 'Alba Luxurians'
Clematis cirrhosa var. *balearica*
Clematis viticella
Cobaea scandens
Dicentra macrocapnos
Lathyrus latifolius 'White Pearl'
Rosa 'Félicité et Perpétue'

Wall shrubs
Coronilla glauca 'Citrina'
Correa alba
Correa backhousiana
Cytisus × *kewensis*
Cytisus praecox
Forsythia suspensa 'Nymans'
Hydrangea serrata 'Preziosa'
Lonicera fragrantissima
Mahonia haematocarpa
Osmanthus delavayi
Pyracantha 'Golden Charmer'

Trailers
Asarina procumbens
Cymbalaria muralis albiflora
Euphorbia myrsinites
Jasminum parkeri

Shrubs
Abelia × *grandiflora* 'Francis Mason'
Cestrum parqui
Choisya 'Aztec Pearl'
Choisya ternata
Choisya ternata 'Sundance'
Colletia paradoxa
Daphne (in variety)
Euphorbia characias ssp. *wulfenii*
Fuchsia magellanica 'Alba'
Fuchsia 'Hawkshead'
Hamamelis (in variety)
Rosa glauca
Sarcococca hookeriana var. *digyna*
Skimmia ssp.*reevesiana*

Dark leaves
Aeonium arboreum 'Atropurpureum'
Ajuga reptans 'Atropurpurea'
Anthriscus sylvestris 'Raven's Wing'
Cordyline australis 'Purpurea'
Euphorbia dulcis 'Chameleon'
Foeniculum vulgare 'Purpureum'
Heuchera micrantha 'Palace Purple'
Heuchera 'Pewter Moon'
Ophiopogon planiscapus 'Nigrescens'
Oxalis triangularis

Grey leaves
Alchemilla mollis
Artemisia arborescens
Ballota pseudodictamnus
Convolvulus cneorum
Festuca glauca
Helichrysum petiolare
Helichrysum augustifolium

Herbaceous
Acanthus spinosus
Alcea rosea 'Nigra'
Aquilegia chrysantha
Aquilegia vulgaris double black
Arum italicum ssp. *italicum*
Campanula alliariifolia
Campanula takesimana
Darmera peltata
Dicentra spectabilis alba
Euphorbia lathyris
Gaura lindheimeri
Hosta (in variety)
Lychnis coronaria Alba Group
Nicotiana (in variety)
Polemonium pauciflorum
Polyganatum
Saxifraga cuscutiformis
Smilacina racemosa
Thalictrum flavum ssp.*glaucum*
Veratrum nigrum
Verbascum elegantissimum 'Helen Johnson'
Vestia foetida
Yucca filamentosa 'Variegata'
Zantedeschia aethiopica
Zantedeschia aethiopica 'Green Goddess'
Zantedeschia albomaculata 'Black-eyed Beauty'

Bulbs
Arisaema (in variety)
Eucomis (in variety)
Galtonia (in variety)
Tulipa species

The bookshelf

The following books have guided, helped and given me pleasure during the years I have been learning to become a gardener:

BATES, H. E. *A Love of Flowers* Michael Joseph, London 1971

BILLINGTON, JILL *Small Gardens with Style* Ward Lock, London 1994

COMPTON, JAMES *Success with Unusual Plants* Collins, London 1987

FISHER, SUE *Gardeners' World: Plants for Small Gardens* BBC Books, London 1993

GREY-WILSON, CHRISTOPHER, and MATTHEWS, VICTORIA *Gardening on Walls* Collins, London 1983

JOHNSON, A. T., and SMITH, H. A. *Plant Names Simplified* Landsman's Bookshop 1986

JOHNSON, JUDY and BERRY, SUSAN *English Private Gardens* Collins & Brown, London 1991

KELLAWAY, DEBORAH *The Making of Town Gardens* Macmillan, London 1990

KELLY, JOHN *Foliage in Your Garden* Frances Lincoln, London and Viking, New York 1989

LAWSON, ANDREW *Performance Plants* Frances Lincoln, London and Viking, New York 1992

LLOYD CHRISTOPHER *Foliage Plants* Penguin, London 1987
The Well-Tempered Garden Penguin, London 1987

NICOLSON, NIGEL (ed) *Victoria Sackville-West's Garden Book* Michael Joseph 1968

RAVEN, JOHN *A Botanist's Garden* Collins, London 1971

RIX, MARTYN, and PHILLIPS, ROGER *The Bulb Book: a photographic guide to over 800 hardy bulbs* Pan, London 1981

SACKVILLE-WEST, VICTORIA *A Joy of Gardening* (ed H. I. Popper) Harper & Row, New York 1958

Sanders' Encyclopaedia of Gardening (revised A. G. L. Hellyer) Hamlyn, London 1984

THOMAS, GRAHAM STUART *Ornamental Shrubs, Climbers and Bamboos* John Murray, London 1992
Perennial Garden Plants Dent, London 1982
Plants for Ground Cover Dent, London 1982

THOMAS, H. H. *The Book of Hardy Flowers* Cassell, London 1915

VEREY, ROSEMARY *The Garden in Winter* Frances Lincoln, London and New York Graphic Society, New York 1988

Gardens of England and Wales open to the public is published annually under the National Gardens Scheme and known among gardeners as 'The Yellow Book'

The Good Gardens Guide (ed. P. King and G. Rose) is published annually by Vermilion, London

The Reader's Digest Encyclopaedia of Garden Plants and Flowers Reader's Digest Association, London, revised edn 1993

The Plant Finder, published annually by Moorlands Publishing Company, in association with the Hardy Plant Society, lists some 60,000 plants with invaluable information about suppliers and a section on correct nomenclature

Index